SO YOU WANT TO SUCCEED AS A PARENT

SO YOU WANT TO SUCCEED AS A PARENT

CHARLES B. BECKERT

Bookcraft · Salt Lake City, Utah

Library of Congress Catalog Card Number: 82-73310
ISBN 0-88494-468-9

First Printing, 1982

Lithographed in the United States of America
PUBLISHERS PRESS
Salt Lake City, Utah

Contents

Acknowledgments

I wish to express my thanks to my wife, Olga, for her continued encouragement and support as I wrote the manuscript; my four sons, Bartley, Daniel, Troy, and Lance, for the many father-son experiences we have shared; my parents, Charles and Edna Beckert, and my brothers and sisters, for the positive family environment on which I have drawn for this book; my uncle, Dr. Gaylon L. Caldwell, for his unselfish and beneficial help with the manuscript; an esteemed colleague, Marvin H. Christensen, for his ideas; and the hundreds of parents and children I have been privileged to work with as a teacher, therapist, and friend.

Introduction

You're right! It is another book about parenting. I know library shelves sag under the weight of how-to-be-good-parent titles, and bookstores continue to rake in revenue from their sale. "Why then," you ask, "am I adding yet another to the existing plethora of parenting manuals?" My answer is twofold: first, my avowed goal in life is to help strengthen families, and I honestly think this book will contribute to that aim; second, I've long wanted to write a book. There, you have it.

There are many excellent references available to parents, and I, for one, welcome any additions which will help in this most challenging area of life. The modern proverb "Different strokes for different folks" seems appropriate here. Obviously, not every parent is going to feel totally comfortable with any one particular parenting style or philosophy. One book may be a prize for one individual and a bust for another. My hope is that this book will reach some who have not as yet found what they have been looking for. Perhaps these tidbits of wisdom will "ring bells" and "turn lights on" for interested parents. One of these proverbs may be the key to unlock a chained or strained relationship between parent and child.

I have chosen to bring to the readers the "wisdom of the ages," the uncanonized "oral tradition of the fathers," as it were. Such wisdom as contained in the sayings, proverbs, slogans, mottos, and witticisms handed down from generation to generation has survived because it has value.

I have been collecting these sayings for several years and find them very helpful and inspiring in my life. My intention has been to put these proverbs into a here-and-now family context. Each chapter is intended as a singular gem of wisdom, simple and short enough to be read at one sitting.

At the conclusion of each chapter are some practical suggestions on how to apply the particular information within the family. You will need to pick and choose from those given and find what will help you in your particular circumstances. Don't be fooled by their seeming simplicity. They have worked for others and will work for you.

As parents, we have been given stewardship over some of Heavenly Father's children. It is a sobering and sacred obligation and opportunity.

1

Plan Your Work, and Work Your Plan

There is an important lesson to be learned from the Savior's words in Luke 14:28-30. It is that we need to plan, outline, and blueprint before undertaking any major challenge.

In this passage, Jesus, himself a carpenter, assumes that any thinking person planning even the building of a tower would first sit down and calculate the cost before beginning construction. This is a protection. Only when things are so trivial as not to matter much will any of us begin a project without first having thought it through—without having determined what we intend to accomplish and how we can accomplish it.

For example, only a person with unlimited time on his hands (and gasoline in his tank) would start out without a map and with a firm decision not to pay any attention to directions. Then the final destination would be determined by the interplay of pure chance and mood-of-the-moment choices. Such a trip probably would be an adventure, but very few among us would dedicate even a week to such accidental and unpredictable use of our time.

Certainly, none of us would give a moment's thought to applying this approach to our life plans. It simply would not provide the kind of firm foundation which would give any hope for surviving the storms of life we know will come. If we don't know where we want to go and have some idea how to get there, failure is almost certain.

When we contemplate the extraordinary importance of the first critical years for a child, it really is astonishing how little time and energy many parents devote to planning what they want to achieve and how they expect to realize their aims. Child rearing is a project of enormous consequence; and to be successful, parents need a philosophy of children and their nurture. They must know where they want to end up with their children and how they will get there. Obviously, it is necessary that both parents follow the same blueprint, because only if they agree on a single plan and abide by it will they avoid attempting to travel in two different directions at one time.

Without a philosophy to guide them, parents are like sculptors chiseling away on a stone with little regard for the end result and thinking that as long as they hammer and chip, they are productive and will be satisfied with the final result. The story is told about a stranger who asked Michelangelo how he was able to take a piece of stone and sculpt a *Moses* from it. The artist's answer was simple but profound. He replied, "I simply see the man Moses in my mind and then chisel away all that isn't him."

There are few Michelangelos, but every parent is a sculptor. One poet (whom I have never been able to identify) made this point so unerringly and simply that I have committed the words to memory. Please think about the implications of this little poem for you as a parent:

A Piece of Clay

I took a piece of plastic clay
And idly fashioned it one day,

And as my fingers pressed it still,
It moved and yielded to my will.

I came again when days were past,
The bit of clay was hard at last,
The form I gave it, it still bore,
And I could change that form no more.

I took a piece of living clay,
And gently formed it day by day,
And molded with my power and art,
A young child's soft and yielding heart.

I came again when years were gone,
It was a man I looked upon;
He still that early impress wore,
And I could change him never more.

Of course, children are not clay, and the "molding" we do in their early years has to take account of differing spiritual and personal attributes each may well have brought with him from the premortal life. I am a bit uncomfortable too with the final line of the poem, because I do believe in the basic ability of humankind to change. Perhaps the poet meant that once the malleable years are over, only the person concerned can make changes. If so, the responsibility for us early molders becomes the more awesome because the opportunities we once had will pass. In any event, it is easy to agree with the old maxim that "the child is father to the man." And to accept this helps parents understand the immensity of their task.

I am convinced that as parents we have been given stewardship of our children by our Father in Heaven. This is a creative role in his plan; and, like the Great Creator of all, who created all things spiritually before creating them naturally (see Moses 3:5), we should pay attention first to the spiritual before focusing on the physical aspects of child nurture. This means that we need a blueprint to follow as we strive to fulfill our sacred stewardship. Such a plan will be most successful if it represents the thoughts and feelings of both father and mother. Fashioning a mutually acceptable philosophy of child rearing is not easy, but it is within the capabilities of every person God has entrusted with children. To "plan your work, and work your plan" in the parental role requires emotional awareness and honesty, effective communication, and a willingness to expend sincere and continuous effort. Remember, the infant is God's gift to parents, and the grown man or woman is the parent's gift back to God.

SUGGESTIONS:

1. I suggest that parents and parents to be formulate a plan for rearing children. It is essential that father and mother do this together to insure consistency for the child. Parents cannot dictate nor guarantee a child's destination, but they can supply the child with desirable and acceptable opportunities and alternatives. I suggest that each spouse, independently of one another, answer this question in writing: "What do I want my child to have?" You may find the following questions as useful guides for this exercise. Once both of you have expressed yourselves, you should compare responses. A discussion will certainly follow, and it is hoped that you will decide upon some mutually agreeable goals.

—What kinds of rights should children have?
—How much freedom should children have?
—How much privacy should children have?
—How much voice should children have in family matters?
—How and when should children be disciplined?
—How much responsibility should parents assume for the behavior of their children?
—How self-reliant should parents expect their children to be?
—How much should parents expect of and from their children?
—What should be the nature of the parent-child relationship?
—If you could give your child five things, other than material items, what would they be? List in order of importance to you.

2. Once a destination is determined, you should formulate a plan on how to get where you want to go. You should decide on a method of travel as well as possible routes to take, remembering

that repairs, modifications, and detours may be necessary along the way. But never lose sight of where you want to go so that you can devise alternative ways to get there. Whenever I am in doubt about what to do, I have found it helpful to ask myself this question: "Will this action get me and the child closer to where we want to go?"

3. Once you have a plan, you must exert all your energies to put it into effect. A plan, regardless of how good it is, is of no value unless it is followed.

2

The Best Thing Parents Can Do for Their Children Is to Love One Another

Here is a question for you, and you have only half a minute to answer: "What is the most important thing parents can do for their children?"

I have asked this many times, and all the replies have convinced me that it is a question people ask themselves frequently. From my experience, the most common response is, "We need to love the child." Another favorite is, "We need to provide for the fulfillment of the child's needs." "To allow the child space and opportunity for individual growth and development" is another frequent answer. I certainly cannot argue against any of these replies, for each of them is of the utmost importance. What I want to do is suggest an idea to you that doesn't surface very often; in fact, people seldom mention it.

What I have in mind is not something done to the child directly, but it does provide the youngster with a most crucial experience, one which has major import on the child's life. I'm suggesting that the marriage relationship—the sum total of the feelings and attitudes between the husband and wife—is one of the most important elements in a child's life. The husband-wife relationship is the primary relationship in the family system, and many marriages fail because this principle is not always recognized and adhered to.

Much too often being a good father or mother becomes more important than being a good husband or wife. This emphasis often appears even in the Church curriculum. A brief review of the lessons and study materials for both Priesthood and Relief Society indicates that parenting skills are more often the topic of discussion than are marriage skills. Perhaps marriage skills are assumed, but I am convinced that a good marriage requires a great deal of conscious and constant effort. In my opinion, if we were to spend more time and energy on developing and maintaining a healthy marriage relationship, we would encounter fewer parenting problems. Prevention is still more valuable and more effective than rehabilitation.

There are several scriptural references such as Ephesians 5:31, which state plainly that a man should leave his father and mother and "shall be joined unto his wife and they two shall be one flesh." We know that the marriage relationship endures throughout eternity. And although we also know that "families are forever" and that the members are sealed as a unit, still we also expect (and hope) that our children will leave us someday and form their own families. I am not suggesting that family oneness isn't important, but I do want to emphasize that we must make sure we do not allow our parents, our in-laws, or even our children to divide us as parent partners.

In the D&C 42:22 the Lord counsels us to cleave to our mate and to none else. This is ordinarily interpreted to mean that one should remain faithful to his spouse and not become involved with another adult in an intimate way. But when you think about it, couldn't this modern scripture also be commanding us not to cleave to children or parents to the point of negatively affecting a marriage?

Of course, there are situations when one parent may be so abusive to the children that the mate must step in to protect them, but such cases certainly are exceptions. More often one meets parents (mostly mothers) in therapy who do not willingly accept the counsel of cleaving to one's mate. I understand that these parents feel they are doing what is best for the child; but I'm convinced it is better for the child, in the long run, to be reared in a home where the mother and father are truly united.

President Kimball has stated that parenting should be a *partnership* in the fullest sense of the word. Parents must not only fall in love; they need to stay in love. Their relationship provides the child with a model of getting along with others, in good and bad times. It also serves as the basic source of a child's security. The youngster's attitude toward life tends to depend upon perceptions of how the mother and father get along with each other. Although most children are amazingly adaptable and can adjust to the loss of one or both parents, still they exhibit much more security and feel much better when they sense permanency in their family system.

In therapy it is almost always the case that when parents bring a child in for counseling, the child is nearly forgotten within a few sessions, while the parents have moved into marriage counseling. My own therapeutic experiences have proven the following statement to be true more often than not: "Show me a child in trouble and I'll show you a troubled marriage." In most cases, however, problems of the child disappear as he or she perceives the relationship between the parents becoming stronger and more positive.

Thus, the best thing parents can do for their children is to love one another.

SUGGESTIONS:

1. Sit down with your spouse and evaluate your relationship. Do your best to view it from your child's frame of reference. Analyze the kind of a "show and tell" drama the two of you portray on a screen much larger, more real, and infinitely more impressive than cinemascope.

2. You may want to elicit the assistance of a third party, someone who can view your relationship more objectively than

you can. Remember, self-awareness and self-acceptance must precede change.

3. You may want to look at such areas in your marriage as:
—How are decisions made in our relationship?
—How do we handle basic differences which exist between us?
—How do we accept different personal traits?
—What is our basic attitude toward life and other people?
—How do we demonstrate love, acceptance, and support for each other?
—How do we feel about religion, and what role does it play in our lives?

4. Spend whatever time and energy necessary to strengthen your relationship. You'll be glad you did; and, as a by-product, it will make a significant contribution to the emotional well-being of your child.

3

Nobody Cares How Much You Know Until They Know How Much You Care

---

The majority of the parents I encounter in my work really are dedicated to helping their children. They want to provide proper guidance; they are prepared to do whatever they can to give their child a good life, even a better life than they have perceived themselves to have had. Because they want the best for their children, some even take special classes. The fact that they make appointments with me or, like you, are reading this book, is adequate proof that they take their responsibilities very seriously.

I am pleased that they are doing this. If anything, more parents should dedicate more time to the science and art of parenting. But I become concerned when some of them place all their reliance on obtaining pure knowledge or seek a system for applying principles and ideas, because I do not believe that the most important key to positive parenting is the acquisition of knowledge. The title to this chapter makes the point that the personal relationship parents have with their children will result in a greater impact on that child than all the knowledge in the world.

Most people will accept as true the popular saying "Knowledge is power." But it is more applicable in some situations than in others, and this is especially the case if knowledge (which is measured by many in college degrees) is automatically assumed to result in wisdom. If some people read this book with greater concentration and increased confidence because the author has a doctorate in the field of marriage and family therapy, so be it. They are like the lady who registered for a semester class in psychology for parents which I was teaching. During the initial session when I asked the members why they had signed up for the course and what they expected to get out of it, she said, "I knew I was having some problems with my little boy, and when I saw that this class was offered and was to be taught by a Ph.D., I knew it would help me understand my son better." I did my best not to disappoint her.

But I was more impressed at a fireside presentation when one man, in response to my asking if anyone had any questions, stood up and asked, "What are your qualifications and credentials to be telling us how to have better families?" He really was concerned about *wisdom* rather than *knowledge* and was satisfied when I told him that I had been very happily married for twenty years and was the father of four sons, three of whom were teenagers. Apparently he knew that the evening's presentation was not going to be one of those occasions when (as my mother used to say) "the old maid tells people how to raise their children." He had no objection to my Ph.D. (and was even happier when he discovered I had earned it from Brigham Young University, "the Lord's school," as he called it).

My experience makes it very plain that the younger generation is not nearly as impressed by what we know or how we learned it as are their elders. Most young people are much more impressed by how they think we feel toward them.

Parents need to realize that their personal relationships with a child will have more impact on that child than all the knowledge they can obtain. The primary concern of every very young person is to be accepted and loved. Once children have this sense of security, they will listen much more attentively to what parents, teachers, and other adults tell them. After positive relationships have been established, the application of knowledge begins to have power with children—but only then. Learning is much easier and more effective in an atmosphere of love and acceptance.

The words of Jacob in 2 Nephi 9:28-29 affirm this point. He said: "Oh the vainness, and the frailties, and the foolishness of men! When they are learned they think they are wise, and they hearken not unto the counsel of God, for they set it aside, supposing they know of themselves, wherefore, their wisdom is foolishness and it profiteth them not. And they shall perish. But to be learned is good if they hearken to the counsels of God."

In the spirit of Jacob's words, we need to be sure that our priorities are right. I recently read a study which disclosed that the average father spends less than twelve minutes each day alone with his child. This statistic has the mark of tragedy. Every such "average father" ought to reexamine his priorities, remembering the great insight of President David O. McKay that "No other success can compensate for failure in the home."

The meaning of this for you and me is that we can teach the knowledge we obtain only to those who trust us. The first foundation stone of trust is the belief that we really care about our children. Children are perceptive: To them our actions speak louder than our words, and they understand our examples much more easily than our words.

SUGGESTIONS:

1. Find the opportunity each day to make sure that each child knows he or she is loved, respected, valued, important, cherished, worthwhile. Do anything that will send the message that you really care.

2. It is not enough to tell the child: Demonstrate your feelings so there is no question that he or she is loved and accepted—unconditionally.

3. It may be helpful for you to keep a record for the first little while of each time you "validate" your child. Let me explain briefly this "validation" idea. One day upon entering a large commercial parking lot, I was given a piece of paper which in and of itself had

no real value. The attendant said that if one of the neighboring businesses would validate the ticket, I would not have to pay for parking. If not, it would cost one dollar for the first hour and fifty cents for each additional one. In other words, the ticket had no value unless stamped by someone who was significant. I did make a purchase that day, and a young lady stamped *valid* on my parking stub. Only now was the paper of value to me and accepted by the parking attendant.

Since thinking about that experience, I have determined to find some way each and every day to "validate" each member of our family. Maybe the "stamp" is in the form of a hug or a kiss. Perhaps it is a spoken word of love and acceptance. However I "validate" my children or my mate each day, they know they are of value to me. They are convinced that I really do care about them.

4

Children Are Born Through Us, Not to Us

Some years ago a graduate professor made the statement that is the subject of this chapter. He said it while making a sweeping motion with his hands, moving them from high above his head downward and then out and away from his stomach. His action suggested a profound principle: Children come *through* the parents. My own conviction is that each child comes from a heavenly parent to an earthly parent who has the obligation to nourish, train, and then send the child out into the world prepared to continue the cycle.

There are those who believe otherwise, but the process of the child's coming through the parents doesn't change—only the concept of the original source is different. Thus, we don't have to share a conviction regarding a heavenly parent in order to agree that the primary objective of parenthood is to prepare each child to function without the parents. I am confident that every thoughtful parent will accept this principle.

The Lord has given parents some definite challenges and directions as to what they should provide for his children here on earth, especially while they are young. King Benjamin did not mince words when he declared: "And ye will not suffer your children that they go hungry, or naked; neither will ye suffer that they transgress the laws of God, and fight and quarrel one with another, and serve the devil.... But ye will teach them to walk in the ways of truth and soberness; ye will teach them to love one another, and to serve one another" (Mosiah 4:14-15). In another place the Lord stresses the importance of teaching children the spiritual, soul-saving truths of the gospel (D & C 68:25-27). The point is that all of these instructions are designed to help the child gain the physical, social, emotional, and spiritual strength necessary to survive on his own.

Please don't think that I am suggesting a child be sent away at the earliest possible age, or even that parents need feel no responsibility for the child throughout life. What I affirm is that the child is a separate entity, a person with a destiny of his own. The overriding parental obligation is to launch a confident child on the search for ultimate independence and success.

After a good deal of clinical experience, I have come to feel extremely sorry for any child who, no matter what the reasons, is so tightly tied to his parents that he does not want to leave the nest. I grieve for the young person who can't make a decision without directly involving the parents. It is tragic when a child grows up afraid of the world or of making decisions and when he must constantly have the intimate companionship of parents.

Even more pitiable is the parent who cannot cut a child loose and so enjoy the glorious day when children become adult friends. I am convinced that parents harm rather than help a child by seeking constantly to fulfill every wish and need of a son or daughter. This not only fails to recognize the potential strengths and capabilities of a child, but also actually prevents development of them. Saddest of all is the parent who regards the child as a possession. An owner is totally responsible for possessions, and if children are considered to be owned, then the parent becomes personally responsible for everything the child does. This places both parties in a helpless situation.

We constantly need to remind ourselves that children are not *things* to be owned or used, but rather *individuals* to be nurtured, given direction, and then allowed to live their own lives. My professor was right: Children are born through parents and not to them.

SUGGESTIONS:

1. Take enough time to allow uninterrupted thinking about your attitude relative to this motto. Make a list of those things you do that indicate a desire to run a child's life. If you identify such behaviors, make a commitment and a plan to abandon such actions.

2. As you strive to eliminate any destructive behaviors, find ways to demonstrate to the child that you regard him as an individual who someday will be on his own. One way to accomplish this is to give the child increasing responsibilities commensurate with his age and ability. In addition, the topic of eventual departure from the nest should be discussed from time to time as a natural step—but please, never as a threat.

3. Continually teach each little individual that he is involved in a progressive cycle of childhood/parenthood and has a destiny to fulfill.

5

Mind Your Own Business

About a year ago a very angry and disturbed fifteen-year-old boy was referred to me for help. It seems he wanted to get rid of his mother. This was his avowed goal, and he even talked about how he was going to take her life. The authorities couldn't do much about it because he never tried to carry out his threats. He was, however, driving her out of her mind. The boy did not want therapy, but because he was on probation for smoking dope and burglarizing, family counseling was required, or he would be taken from the home. In spite of the threats and constant emotional pressure, the parents wanted to keep their son at home as long as they could.

I chose to see the boy (we'll call him Matt), his mother, and his father together in the initial session. During this first meeting, it immediately became evident that the father stood between his wife and son. The relationship between Matt and his dad seemed to be open at least, and it was apparent that some empathy existed. Between Matt and his mom, however, only hostility and hurt came out. It has always been painful for me to be faced with family problems in which one parent uses the other to fight his battles.

The family members were told to decide for themselves how they wanted to sit; and, not surprisingly, the father placed himself between the other two, the buffer between the two enemies. The basic theme of that counseling session emerged as if according to a prearranged battle plan: Mom would accuse and dig at Matt, who would respond with threats of violence.

I obtained a great deal of information from the first session regarding the relationship within the family system and the rules which governed the action. A week or so later I had the opportunity to talk with Matt alone. I wanted him to tell me about his life. He really was an angry boy. It didn't matter that most of his goals were apparently unrealistic; it was important that his anger was less noticeable when talking about the future. Whenever the subject of his mother came up, however, his voice would raise, taking on a bitter, hostile quality. I encouraged Matt to review his past life, especially his interactions with his mother. As he talked, a plain pattern began to emerge. What I perceived was the familiar description of an overprotective (i.e., "too good") mother. She did everything for Matt and the other children. She had absolutely no doubt that she was doing the best thing for them by protecting them from the world. She interfered in their interpersonal relationships when things weren't going well. She did homework for them when it was almost due and not yet done. She made decisions for them at every level. And, to top it off, she became very much involved in their personal lives. Matt told me in one of our sessions that his mother knew everything, literally *everything*, about him. He had no secrets, no privacy from her and, in fact, he had never had any. (She told me herself that she felt so responsible for Matt that she believed she had the right and duty to invade his world.) She would inspect his room, suspecting the worst, such as drugs or other contraband; she listened in on his phone calls; she read his mail and notes as she would find them. Matt described her as the best prosecuting attorney the world would ever know. Her questioning techniques, pressure, and intensity were overwhelming. Matt was convinced that she could make anyone crack.

To put it briefly: She had invaded Matt's life space, and he hated her for it. While her intentions may have been the best, her accusations and insinuations motivated Matt to act them out in many instances. I am not and cannot excuse the boy for his many wrong choices in handling his problems, nor for his quickness in blaming his mother for everything. But I am pointing out that Matt certainly felt justified in doing what he was doing because of her actions. He felt he had to get back at her one way or another.

The point is that everyone must have the right to some privacy. No one desires to be fully exposed—neither children nor parents. Each person has his life space; and when attempts are made to break into it uninvited, resistance will come in an effort to maintain some individual integrity.

A simple analogy will illustrate this point. A life can be compared to a home. Suppose you have a nice house, complete with front porch and all the essential rooms. Among those rooms, some are more personal than others for you. For example, the front porch of the house is pretty much accessible to anyone who cares to walk up the steps. Most often a stranger will be left on the porch, even after requesting entrance, if he is selling something you are not interested in. Should he attempt to force his way into your house the police will protect your castle.

Suppose the person knocking on your door is someone you know a bit better. You will likely allow him into the living room but probably nowhere else. As your trust deepens for the individual, you may ask him or her into the kitchen. If this person feels close enough to you, you may receive (and grant) a request to use your bathroom. An average person would not just walk into the bathroom, and if one did, you probably would feel offended. The reason why is that each different room tends to have more and more personal meaning for you. One usually must know a person, even an adult of the same sex, very well before showing him the bedroom. That's how it is in our own lives. We need to structure some privacy. All of us need some things which are just ours.

Children are no different from adults in this way. How would you like someone reading your mail or perhaps your diary without permission? How would you like to find out someone had been eavesdropping on your personal phone calls? Or rummaging through your closets and drawers?

Some parents invade the privacy of their children under the guise of personal ownership of the child. Perhaps you have heard some parent scream at her daughter, "You're my child, and I'll do with you whatever I want!" This simply is not so. Children are not the possessions of their parents; neither are they mere extensions of them. Children are individuals, persons with certain rights. Parents are responsible for their children, but they do not own them.

I once overheard two adults talking. One said something to the other, who in turn raised his voice in response. The first then asked, "Why are you so defensive?" I could have explained why the second person was defensive. He felt under attack. People feel the need to defend themselves when they are afraid for their well-being, whether it be emotional or physical.

Children often react so defensively because they feel they are about to be invaded or overrun.

I have talked with literally hundreds of teenagers who have admitted to certain accusations not because they were guilty, but because it was the only way they knew to get a parent (or parents) "off their backs," as they put it. I distinctly remember one young lady responding to her accusing father with these words, "What do you want me to say?" You see, he was breaking into her space, and she didn't want him to do it. Young people frequently are defending themselves the only way they know how. In our society acting in self-defense is acceptable behavior more often than not.

So what can parents do? How does an interested parent find out about a child's life and thoughts? This is important because knowing one's child better certainly improves the odds of being a better parent. There are three basic ways to get into someone's life space. Of these, two will almost always backfire, causing a break in the relationship.

The first way, intrusion, from the verb intrude, means to break in or through, to enter when not wanted. Intrusion into another's life space will destroy the relationship and trust. Intrusive behavior will be met by resistance, either passively or actively.

The second way, encroachment, is used here as it applies to football. It is a rule violation and occurs when one player lines up on the wrong side of the ball. He fudges. He doesn't crash across the line, but he takes advantage of the other person by lining up in his space. Encroachment occurs in life when one listens in, reads private notes, or plays the role of a spy. It is sneaky.

The third way is the only proper way "in"; and it is by invitation. If an individual trusts us, the desire to share something with us will follow. We are welcome to his space, at least within the limits the host establishes. Such invitations come when relationships are positive and trustworthy. If you don't crowd, someday an eight-year-old will show you his secret hiding place. If you don't push, maybe that silent teenager will let you in on some of those special thoughts, doubts, and feelings experienced in that precious yet turbulent age. If you remember to mind your own business you will have a much better chance to become a consultant or advisor to your child's business. Patience is the key. And as the child grows older, you should fight even more the urge to "help" unless your assistance is requested.

SUGGESTIONS:

1. Discuss the right to privacy in the home with the entire family.

2. Allow each person—parents and children—to have a secret and private place, whether a closet, drawer, or merely a box. All should understand what is off-limits.

3. Concentrate always on building a relationship of trust and understanding with one another.

4. Ask for permission to enter another's space (room, letter, information, head or heart).

5. Allow the children to suffer the consequences of their behavior. Don't always protect them because you think you own them; it is better to have them ask for your help.

6

Rewarded Behavior Continues

The topic of this chapter is one of the least complex principles in psychology and yet one of the most useful. It is an effective key to understanding and changing behavior in ourselves as well as in our children. All you need to remember is: Rewarded behavior continues.

"Why do I do what I do?" is one of the most poignant and yet most often asked of all questions. There are two basic schools of thought about it. One theory is past oriented. Its champions maintain that our experiences from the past determine our behavior in the present. They believe that behavior is caused. I'm certain that there is some truth in this concept, but I cannot accept it as the sole explanation. Such determinism denies free agency, as well as leaves no opportunity for change. It is impossible for me or anyone else to change history and that is what past behavior is—history.

A competing theory of "Why I do what I do" is present and future oriented. Advocates of this concept insist that we do things in an attempt to fulfill some need or purpose. They maintain that behavior is purposeful, as contrasted to being caused. To be purposeful means it is goal oriented. The past is important because we have learned what we need to do in order to reach particular goals.

I line up with those who consider that behavior is, in general, purposeful. I think the principle that we act in order to reach certain goals or to obtain certain rewards (payoffs) operates from infancy on. All of us learn what to do in order to get what we want, and that is why psychologists label it learned behavior. For example, we realize early that if we cry a certain way, we can get attention and services from those around us. If someone comes to our assistance when we cry, it is obvious that we will continue the practice of crying whenever we desire attention.

Students will work hard for an *A* or a *B* if a good grade is a valued reward for them. If, however, good grades are important to *parents,* a student who wishes to upset his parents may choose to do very poorly in school. His reward in this case is the negative one of upsetting (or controlling) the parents.

The theory holds that we select behavior we believe will get us what we want at a particular time. Therefore, the crying infant and the hardworking (or nonworking) student are following the same principle as the person who goes to work day after day in order to receive his rewards—a paycheck generally being first among them. Of course, we may not be entirely aware of what the real rewards are from a particular behavior we have learned to utilize. In some cases the avoidance of pain is the reward sought.

Church activity or inactivity furnishes an interesting application of this theory. People attend church and participate as long as they find it rewarding. Should it become less rewarding than something else, or even painful, they will change their behavior regarding church services. (Some may choose to attend church, even though it may be painful, to avoid the even greater fear of offending God.) Many will be active or inactive for a wide variety of reasons, but this psychological theory assures us that these can be understood from a careful analysis.

For example, if a number of students stopped attending Sunday

School classes, the dedicated teacher naturally would make every effort to find out why. The behavior-is-purposeful position narrows the causes of their ditching down to one of two reasons: 1) the class has become unrewarding or at worst painful, or 2) they have found something more rewarding (ranging from the negative reward of upsetting parents to the positive pleasure of dunking doughnuts at Winchell's).

Those who fail to receive the expected reward from a specific behavior will switch to another type of conduct. For example, since people work for rewards, an employee who receives neither wage increases, a sense of contributing, nor the other kinds of compensation expected will likely look for employment elsewhere and certainly will do so if the monetary payoff isn't forthcoming. The same thing is true for a baby. If crying fails to bring someone to take care of his needs, the infant finds another means (behavior) to attract attention. This may be thumb sucking, whining, or bed-wetting. A child might even learn to talk and actually express what is wanted.

If we apply the motto of this chapter to any of these situations in an effort to influence or change the behavior of a child, we first must determine what the reward is for that behavior. By removing the payoff and/or providing a more positive reward for the behavior we desire, the conduct of the child will be influenced.

Doing this isn't as easy as may appear at first glance. Often it is difficult to determine accurately what reward is sought by a particular negative behavior. But this much is certain: If a specific behavior continues there is somewhere a reward in it for the person. If the behavior is unacceptable to the parent, the associated reward must be determined and removed. Perhaps outside help will be needed in order to locate the real payoff and to substitute a positive one.

I'm suggesting that if you've tried to alter a child's negative behavior with a certain reaction and the behavior is still going on, your very reaction may be providing the child with the reward. Try changing your reaction, thus forcing the child to change his approach. When the child's behavior becomes acceptable, it should be quickly rewarded, thus encouraging its continuation. Be patient.

The plan will really work. Rewarded behavior will continue. Be certain, however, that the reward is of value to the child, not just to you. If the child does not want the reward offered, he will not be motivated to change or continue the behavior.

SUGGESTIONS (to stop negative behavior):
1. Identify and describe what the unacceptable behavior is.
2. Determine what reward or payoff the child receives for the behavior.
3. Remove the payoff, and the behavior should begin to slack off.
4. If the behavior doesn't change, look for another payoff and remove it, repeating the process as necessary.

I hasten to add that if you choose the correct payoff and remove it, the behavior of the child will get worse before it improves. Don't reject the system too early, and your patience will be rewarded.

SUGGESTIONS (to encourage positive behavior):
1. Identify and describe the positive behavior you desire.
2. Provide a reward for the child each time the desired behavior occurs. Make sure the payoff is something of value to the child.
3. Continue to reinforce the behavior, every time at first and then just often enough to maintain it. (Think about how the slot machines in Las Vegas are designed to work—intermittent reinforcement is all it takes.)

7

To Me, Whatever I Do Is the Best Thing to Do at the Time That I Do It

Of all the mottos I have read, collected, and used, the motto "To me, whatever I do is the best thing to do at the time that I do it" has been the most beneficial in my life. Even so, I doubt if any motto has been more difficult to explain to others. Some people, like me, have a very hard time understanding it, but once they do, they feel a great relief.

The motto brings deliverance because it makes possible accepting what others have done, although you may disagree with or even have difficulty tolerating their behavior. The motto sets you free to say truthfully such a profound statement as, "If I had been in your shoes and had felt the way you felt and had thought the way you were thinking, I very likely would have done exactly what you did." In brief, the motto frees us to accept others and to understand why they do what they do.

I am convinced that behavior is purposeful, that is, people do something to satisfy some need or to realize some goal. For example, consider the child who gets out of bed at 10 P.M. complaining that he needs a drink of water. The youngster really may be thirsty. If so, the sensible thing to fulfill this need is to ask for a drink. On the other hand, the youngster may just want attention. The "I-want-a-drink" routine is a scheme hatched in the little mind to reach a goal. In either case, the behavior is purposeful. Before the familiar sentence is uttered, the child is convinced, consciously or subconsciously, that asking for a drink is the thing to say. The timing may be very poor (and if it is the tot may end up with something far worse than thirst); nevertheless, when the child asked for water it seemed to him the best thing to do.

I am not suggesting that all behavior is acceptable just because someone considers that an action seems to be appropriate at the time. Some conduct is unmistakably wrong and ought not to be shrugged off. For instance, showing disrespect for a teacher or tearing up a note which should have been brought home ought not to be ignored. What I mean is that we should understand that the child believed the behavior to be appropriate at the time. If we begin with this assumption, we will be in the kind of calm emotional state which encourages looking back and attempting to find out what need the wrong action was intended to fulfill or what goal it gave promise of attaining. Once armed with this understanding, we are in a much better position to take necessary steps to help someone see that his behavior really was a bad idea.

A morsel of biblical wisdom which has long intrigued me states, "The way of a fool is right in his own eyes" (Proverbs 12:15). This explains why arguments and differences of opinion can hang on and on. Even if both parties have behaved foolishly, both are "right" in their own eyes. And, if they could miraculously change places, attitudes, and experiences with the other party, each would continue to disagree, but on reverse sides.

What does this mean to you and me? As a parent, a teacher, and a friend, my real challenge is to understand the *why* of behavior *before* I attempt to change it. This is particularly important when children are concerned. Once we acknowledge to ourselves that we probably would have done the same thing had we been in their shoes, we will not become upset. Instead, rather than labeling and rejecting our children, we will take the time and effort necessary to guide them to more appropriate behavior. It is a motto which offers greater and more certain dividends than any investment plan I know.

SUGGESTIONS:

1. Think back over your past and write down some of the dumb things you have done. Then put yourself back in your shoes at the time of those decisions and help yourself to realize that under the same circumstances, without the knowledge you now have, you would do the same things again.

2. The next time you are about to react negatively to a particular behavior, stop and repeat this motto to yourself. Then do your best to understand the situation before you react to it.

8

Only a Discouraged Child Misbehaves

Experience has taught me that the word *discouragement* has a different meaning for each person, thus needing definition each time it is used. Most people think they understand it. But pin them down, and they are often hard pressed to give a specific and clear explanation. For the purpose of this chapter, we will define *discouragement* as "the bad feeling we get when our physical and/or emotional needs and desires are not met."

Another way to define discouragement is to compare it to its opposite, encouragement. When people are encouraged they feel good. Things seem to go their way. They are happy and satisfied. Their needs are fulfilled, and they have hope and faith in the future.

As you can see, encouragement occurs when our needs are fulfilled, and discouragement is evident when these needs go unfulfilled. The key term is *needs*. We all have them. Each psychologist has his own list of needs. For our purposes, we can divide our needs into two basic categories: physical and emotional.

Our physical needs might be defined as food, water, rest, and safety. Certainly if we are hungry enough, thirsty enough, fatigued enough, or frightened enough, we will choose to behave in any manner necessary to satisfy these needs and so stay alive. People have even been known to resort to cannibalism to avoid starvation.

We react similarly to a deprivation of our emotional needs: belonging and feeling competent and useful. Every child, and adult as well, becomes discouraged when these needs are not met and at that time may choose to behave in any manner necessary to fulfill them, just as is the case with the physical needs. When our needs are unmet, most of us focus on the ends rather than the means to achieve those ends.

If a child feels he belongs, is competent in some area, and is of value to others, he will feel good and positive about himself and those around him. In such a situation, the child will not find it necessary to do wrong things in order to get what is needed.

This concept can be understood when we look closely at the type of child who normally misbehaves. This is generally the classroom misfit, the unpopular, the unathletic, the untalented individual. This type chooses friends who feel much the same way about themselves, and together they feed one another the poisons of discouragement.

In case you suddenly begin thinking of those apparently popular kids you know who still get into trouble, let me quickly stipulate that everything is not as it appears on the outside. Many very popular kids in the school still feel lonely, still know discouragement. The same is true about athletes or musicians if they feel they are popular and worthwhile only because of their particular talent.

The other kids, the ones who seem to have it all together, don't need to cause problems or get into trouble in order to feel accepted, competent, and worthwhile.

Some time ago, as an example, a family returned home from a trip out of state. They found, to their dismay, that their home and yard had been "toilet papered," "confettied," and "egged." The family didn't see the mess at its worst because some very kind friends and neighbors had cleaned things up before the owners returned. They learned later who had been responsible for the mess. A young man who had felt a sense of rejection in the neighborhood and church apparently chose to strike out against someone who was well accepted. He was very discouraged and hurt. Had he not been, he would never have felt the need to do what he did.

Anger is a usual outgrowth of discouragement, frustration, and hurt. I think the Apostle Paul had this pattern in mind when he admonished, "Ye fathers, provoke not your children to wrath: but bring them up in the nurture and admonition of the Lord." (Ephesians 6:4.) Children who stay encouraged will more likely stay away from misbehavior and the trouble it causes.

Understanding all of this may appear to make the parents' job quite easy, but it doesn't. Mere understanding never solved a problem. Merely identifying the child's needs and realizing that they are not being met is not enough. The child must be given positive help in fulfilling these needs. Our task is to assist the child in breaking the discouragement cycle which operates in this manner: "I feel negative, and so I do negative things which make me feel more negative and more prone to do negative things," and so on and so on. We want the opposite to occur. It can if a child feels accepted, competent, and worthwhile.

SUGGESTIONS:

1. Be certain the child's physical needs are adequately met. Provide the necessary food, shelter, rest, and water.

2. Validate the child each and every day. Express to your child such statements as, "You know, this family would not be complete without you," or, "Boy, do you add a lot to this family," or, "When you're not at home there seems to be something missing," or, "I'm glad you're part of this family."

3. Recognize the child's accomplishments. We need to make sure the child has opportunities to make, build, bake, create, fix, design, or complete something. He needs to feel successful.

4. Organize family functions so each member has the

opportunity to make a contribution to the family, even if it's taking out the garbage. The fact is that the child is needed if the family is to function at its fullest potential. The feeling of being needed is a great step toward regarding one's self as worthwhile.

5. Write specific plans to organize family functions in such a way that each member can be validated, can feel competent, and worthwhile each day. If it isn't planned, it will not likely happen. Helping people usually doesn't occur by accident.

6. Some families have used the accompanying letter to create an atmosphere of encouragement. In using this letter, each member

---

_____

Dear _____,

I would like to share some personal thoughts and feelings with you at this time. In my opinion, you are a very important part of our family and this family would not be complete without you. You belong with us.

I would also like you to know how much I appreciate all you add to our family. I appreciate you because _____
_____
_____

In addition, I really admire you for _____
_____
_____

I'm glad we are a family and especially happy you are part of it.

Love,

_____

---

of the family would complete and send it to each other member of the family. In a family of seven people, therefore, each individual would receive six letters. The encouragement each receives is astonishing.

When I Fail at a Thing,
I Fail at a Thing, but
I Am Not a Failure

As an experienced baseball
player, I should have realized that nobody gets a hit every time at
bat and this fact should have carried over into every aspect of my
life. But I forgot this once at a critical time in my career and was
discouraged until a real "angel of mercy" (who happened to be my
co-worker) quoted the motto of this chapter to me.

I had experienced a failure with one of my students in
counseling. It seemed vitally important to both of us that I reach
her, but I obviously had not—at least not that time. It is discourag-
ing to fail in a chosen profession when you have worked so hard to
become proficient. My goal was to be a people helper, and I had
been ineffective when my help was needed. This colleague
reminded me of many past successes and challenged me by asking
why I continued to brood over a single negative experience while
apparently forgetting the many positive ones.

It was a real sense of freedom to be forced to view this failure
for what it really was: a single, isolated experience. Just because I

had been unsuccessful in an experience didn't mean I was an unsuccessful person. *I* was not a failure; I had just had *a* failing experience.

Those who decide they are failures because they happen to fail at a particular task will be disinclined to try anything new. Fear of failure is an effective excuse for inaction even though a life without a mixture of hits, runs, and errors would be an extremely boring life.

In the animal kingdom most creatures must prey on others in order to sustain life; and rather than giving up because they fail in the most recent hunt, animals will try again and again. From the beginning, inventive persons haven't despaired easily either. If they had, we would still be rubbing sticks together instead of flipping switches. In the human and animal societies the truth is the same: The only real failure is the one who fails to try again.

Actually, most of us are involved in a wide variety of activities, and we simply can't do them all equally well. Consider the mother who uses dozens of different skills every day. If she burns the beans, that doesn't make her a rotten wife and mother. The same logic applies to the child in school. If he fails an examination, it doesn't mean he is a failure. He is a person who failed at one thing, namely a test. A boy who feels like a failure because he has been cut from an athletic team certainly isn't expected to be joyous, but neither should he erase from his mind all the positive things that have happened to him and the successes he has logged in other areas. Many great athletes have failed at one sport only to excel in another. Consider Babe Ruth as a hitter. He not only led the league and set records with his monumental home runs but also struck out more than any other batter at that time.

Some children choose to travel a different road than the accepted one. This does not mean their parents are failures. And even if parents were inclined to blame themselves because of the wayward child, how do they account for those who were not wayward? At worst, they have failed with *one* child, but they are not total failures.

The point of all this is not to excuse foolish mistakes nor to paper over substantial ones. It is a plea to go on—to continue to function even though we come face-to-face with failure. A sensible person doesn't throw out the entire meal because the soup was cold. Even if we do find that we strike out every time we come to bat, we can "get the picture" and try another sport. In this respect it is vital that both children and adults have realistic expectations. Failure never is fun, and some people court it simply by holding expectations which are too high for them. But at best, we are imperfect beings and we will make mistakes. The important thing is the recognition that whenever we fail at a thing, we fail at *that* thing; we are not failures.

I am a much happier person since I have realized that I don't have to be perfect in all things at all times. As a matter of fact, if we look closely at someone who handles any kind of failure situation poorly, we generally see an individual who measures self-worth by what he can *do*. Therefore, whenever experiences turn out negatively (as they inevitably will), the individual's personal sense of worth is in jeopardy.

Actually the sense of self-worth should have nothing to do with behavior and performance. As a person I am not worth more just because I can play the piano well or golf in the low 70s. Every human being has inestimable worth merely because he or she exists. Our value comes simply from being a child of God.

SUGGESTIONS:
1. Actively listen to a child who has experienced failure. Allow him or her to feel bad about the experience.

2. After emotions have calmed, assure the child you understand how he feels. Let the child know that feeling bad is not wrong, but very natural. To continue to brood over a past situation, however, is of no value. We can't change history.

3. Help the child separate this negative experience from any positive ones. Show the child how to learn from the failure, assuring him that the only real failure is the person who fails to try again.

4. Encourage the child to think about the good experiences of the past and not dwell on those which didn't turn out as desired.

5. Above all, be thou an example of this chapter's motto. Demonstrate what you are telling the child. If this technique fails to bring about the desired effect, *you* are not a failure (nor am I). It is just that the technique didn't work in this situation. We will try again.

10

Never Do for the Child What the Child Can Do for Himself

The proverb "Never do for the child what the child can do for himself" evokes varied responses from parents. Generally, they accept it in theory but fail to implement it in practice. Such behavior indicates that it has not really been accepted by them as a valid working motto.

Based upon my experiences as a family therapist, I can understand that there are several reasons why parents choose to do things for children that children could very well do for themselves. One reason is expedience. Many parents are either not willing, not able, or just too busy or impatient to allow the time it may take for the child to complete a task. The parents often sigh, "It is just easier to do it myself." So they do. I'm referring to any one of a multitude of simple tasks, such as tying shoes, pouring milk, making beds, doing homework, calling friends on the telephone, doing certain yard chores, getting out of an undesirable situation.

Another reason parents do things for a child is to protect the youngster from some kind of hurt. We often label such parenting as overprotective. This parent loves the child so much he is not willing to allow the offspring to fail. It has been correctly observed that some parents are so good, they are bad for their children. Such parents are often shocked and hurt to discover that, in their real efforts to help the child adjust to life, they have actually assisted his maladjustment.

There are also those parents who feel everything should be done as perfectly as possible. They seem unwilling or unable to allow the child an opportunity to accomplish a task because they realize that the youngster will not do it as correctly, as completely, or as neatly as the parents would have done. In these cases the parents often view the child as an extension of themselves. To allow the child to be less than perfect makes the parent see themselves as being less than perfect, a perception they cannot face.

Positive self-esteem is the key to emotional health. In order to function at our highest level, we need to feel good about ourselves. One very good way to build self-esteem is to encounter successful experiences. When we accomplish something, we have a feeling of competency, a sense of being worthwhile, or a pride in contributing.

If, on the other hand, someone does everything for us, we are deprived of those kinds of successful feelings. Unless I do something, I do not have to suffer the consequences: I don't deserve the blame if things go wrong, and I won't get the praise when they go right. Paul, in writing to the Galatians, makes this statement: "But let every man prove his own work, and then shall he have rejoicing in himself alone, and not in another. For every man shall bear his own burden." (Galatians 6:4-5.) If, as a parent, I want my children to grow up assuming responsibility for their behavior, I must allow them to act for themselves.

There are three valid reasons for not doing too much for our children: First, there is a definite negative message communicated when a parent does something for the child that the child could have done for himself. This message simply is, "You can't do it; that's why I'm doing it for you." Even though the parent does not mean to convey this idea, the child will usually perceive it in this way. Second, parents who do too much for the child often create a dependency pattern. The child will expect the parent to continue doing all these things. As most of us can attest, such a pattern results in spoiled, demanding, and pampered children and in relationships which are extremely difficult to alter and correct. The third disadvantage is an obvious (although frequently forgotten) one. It is that parents will not always be around. Someday the child will not have anyone upon whom to rely and may find the need to convert a marriage relationship into a parent-child experience. This naturally has disastrous consequences for many marriages.

As stated in an earlier chapter, we must realize and accept that children are born through us, rather than to us. Our challenge literally is to raise our children so that they can get along without us.

SUGGESTIONS:

1. Before doing something for your child, ask yourself this question: "Could my child do this if I weren't here?" If the answer is affirmative, move out of the way, bite your tongue, and let the child handle it.

2. Allow adequate time for your child to perform tasks within his competence so that you will not feel it necessary to do them.

3. Keep a journal of your child's ability to accomplish tasks. You will probably be surprised to realize how capable your youngster is and how he can tackle progressively difficult tasks with confidence.

11

Take Time for Training

"Take time for training" is a motto that reminds me of my first day as a new tenth-grade seminary teacher. It had been a very frustrating early morning. I had arrived at the seminary around five A.M. to put the final preparations on the first lesson of my new career. During the previous week I had attended the assigned meetings which dealt with roll-book procedures, class announcements, what to do in case of fire, and so on. Nowhere in that endless agenda was there time set aside to help me become a good teacher, especially for what seemed to me to be the critically important first day.

Now I was getting ready to face the students for the first time, and I was more than a little anxious. As the hour came closer and closer I approached one teacher after another, searching for any golden suggestions I could find. But they all assured me that everything would be fine and not to worry. Their comments not only failed to help me, but made me feel even less prepared. I thought that I must be very inadequate to be the only one suffering this way.

Finally the hour arrived, and I stood facing thirty-five bright-eyed, enthusiastic, talkative teenagers. It was then I realized what I was feeling: fear. I was afraid I would be unable to live up to the expectations of those around me or even to my own expectations. I felt unprepared and untrained. I had been taught many things pertaining to teaching, except to teach. Everyone just seemed to assume that I would know what to do.

Needless to say, I survived, but certainly not without a lot of pain. I wish, even now, twenty years of teaching experience later, that those responsible had offered me more specific training in regard to what they expected. I experienced this same frightening feeling of being unprepared and untrained at the birth of our first child. The doctors just expected us to know what to do.

I know we can't be totally trained in all aspects of a particular assignment, but I am certainly more at ease and function better when I am aware of two basic things: First, I like to know what is expected of me. I don't want to have to be a mind reader. Second, I would like some training about how to accomplish the task before me. I can get by with less training if I feel there is going to be ample allowance for error. Otherwise, I become somewhat frightened.

With regard to raising children, one of the most frustrating experiences for both parent and child occurs when a parent expects a child to accomplish something, and the child is not only unaware of what ought to be done but may not know how to do it, even while understanding that he should.

Let me give you a personal example of such a frustration. Arriving home from work some time ago and driving into the carport, I couldn't help but notice all the junk and debris collected there. This is a problem at our home, and it becomes especially bothersome when the wind is a little stronger than usual. I told myself there was no reason for this mess—the boys should have cleaned it up. Certainly they had seen the clutter when they came home from school, just as I did. Like me, they would have had to wade through it to get to the door.

With these thoughts on my mind, I walked into the house. There, all over the family room, were our four boys watching TV as if nothing were wrong. I can still see their surprised faces when I let them have it about the junky carport. I'm convinced now that they really hadn't seen the mess. They had just walked through it.

Our boys are generally obedient and usually do what they are asked without a lot of trouble. Had I expressed to them my expectations about cleaning the carport and explained where to put some of the junk, I am certain that they would have done it. My mistake was expecting them to see exactly what I was seeing and in exactly the same way.

Often parents expect children to respond as adults. In fact, we sometimes look at youngsters as miniature adults, which they certainly are not. They are children and have had only limited experiences in life. They can't know all that we know, and we make a serious mistake if we expect otherwise.

Children, parents, and husbands and wives need to be trained. We all need to be made aware of what is expected. For example, Saturday mornings once were very frustrating for me. I would get up early enough to get my jogging in and then be ready to help around the house until time to leave for the counseling clinic in the early afternoon. I sincerely desired to be of some help to my wife, but things didn't seem to be working out too well. I would ask what I could do to help. She would reply, "Whatever needs to be done."

I would respond, "Well, what needs to be done?"

To which she would counter, "If you can't see what needs to be done and I have to tell you everything, it's easier to do it myself."

At this point I would become frustrated because I honestly did want to be of some assistance, and I really didn't know what to do. I could understand her not wanting to have to treat me as another child, but that insight didn't solve the dilemma.

Finally we sat down, both of us realizing that neither was satisfied with the situation. We talked things over and reached a negotiated compromise, an alternative which seemed mutually acceptable. Our plan was rather simple: She would make a list of jobs needing attention. She lovingly called it her "Honey-Do List." I would decide which of the tasks on the list I would do and in what order. I was satisfied because I knew what I could do to help; she was happy because she didn't have to follow me around all morning telling me what to do, along with when and how. This was a happy ending because someone took time for training. We have used this plan since that time, and it continues to be of great value, even though I now see many of the things that need to be done without having her put them on the list.

What is more frustrating than a job with no job description or basic instructions? What is more unnerving than sitting through a college course and having to "crystal ball" what the instructor is expecting? It is no different with our children. We need to take time for their training.

Four levels of training from least effective to most effective have been described. The least effective level is to *expect* the job to be done without any real training or explanation. The second level is to *tell* the individual what to do and perhaps how to do it. The third level is to *show* him how to do what was expected. The fourth and most effective level is not only to tell and show but to allow the person to *participate* in doing it. Taking the time to train properly within our families will make both parents and children happier.

It is generally easier to learn to do something the right way the first time than to have to unlearn it and then relearn it. It is also true that low self-esteem generally traces back to unrealistic expectations and almost always results in failing experiences. This is true for tasks as varied as putting on shoes to driving power mowers and cars.

SUGGESTIONS:

1. Strive to give the child distinct and specific descriptions of what you would like done. The younger the child, the simpler and more specific the tasks should be. (When you have the time, read 1 Corinthians 14:1-9 and apply it to parents talking with their children. The key is to learn to give a "certain sound.")

2. Analyze the kind of expectations you have for each of your children. Adjust the expectations where necessary to make them realistic.

3. Make sure that you are available to teach and train your children for expected tasks. This requires a planned schedule.

4. Get into the habit of checking with the children to determine if your directions have been understood, or if they have any questions as to what they should do or how they should do a task. They usually will not mind repeating your directions when asked to do so.

5. Above all, don't force them to be mind readers. They do not and literally cannot second guess or even out guess you.

6. If a child is struggling with a particular task, determine if it is a matter of improper or insufficient training rather than the child's attitude problem.

7. Don't feel like a failure if you have to tell a child what needs to be done.

8. Be patient while teaching a child to perform a particular skill. Be willing to break the skill into smaller components if necessary. (The concept of divide and conquer will be discussed at another point.)

9. Remember that at one time in your life, you didn't see the mess or know how to remedy it either.

12

Allow Freedom Within Limits

Whenever parenting is discussed, the matter of setting limits for the child invariably arises. I have encountered a number of parents at both extremes—those who set no limits and those who set many and rigid limits. I also have met those who drift from one extreme to the other, depending upon their mood at the moment, the situation involved, and other circumstances. Most parents line up somewhere between the two extremes.

The first group, those who set no or very few limits, permit the youngster to do as he wishes with little fear of consequences. The other extreme, those parents who set limits which are strict and inflexible, deny the child much to say about his life and practically guarantee that the child will live in constant fear of consequences.

The "drifters" ordinarily excuse themselves as champions of "elastic" limits and argue that these are stretchable depending upon the circumstances. As someone once pointed out, however, "children raised within elastic limits usually have problems in the stretch." Because he can't predict the mood or the explanation of the parents, the child in this situation lives in constant doubt as to what the consequences will be for his actions. Parents who are not at the extremes and yet who don't want to drift generally find it difficult to set and maintain reasonable limits for their children, and so they are the ones who particularly wish to discuss the subject of this chapter.

At the outset, you should know my position: I stand firmly in favor of limits for children. I am convinced that children want and need limits as much as do parents. The child's need for security is paralleled, and often equaled, by the parents' need to feel that things are under control. Both parent and child, it seems to me, function best when order is evident.

An experience I had while working as a teacher and counselor at a state reformatory for boys and girls reinforced my position. Nine teenage girls and I were sitting in a circle and discussing the issue of whether to have definite limits for children within the home. One young lady named Maree expressed her strong resentment of the strict limits her parents had imposed upon her. She actually cursed her mother and accused her of being neither loving nor trusting.

After the hostility had abated somewhat, our attention was diverted to Margo, who sat about three chairs away from Maree. Margo was crying, and no one seemed to know why. Finally, another of the girls managed enough courage to ask Margo what the problem was. Margo stopped sobbing and then turned to Maree. I will never forget her message, and I have a feeling that Maree still remembers it too. Margo said something like this, "Maree, you ought to thank God your mother cared enough for you to set those limits. My mother didn't care what I did, where I went, who I was with, or even if I came home." Maree didn't reply to that particular challenge. But Margo's reaction fortified my conviction that all children want some limits, and most parents do as well.

Actually, it isn't the limits which bother the child so much as the process used to establish them. I'm suggesting for both children and parents that "whatever is imposed is usually opposed," as the saying goes. It is vitally important for parents and their children to work together in setting and maintaining limits for the family. Such parent and child cooperation also should include discussions of the consequences for overstepping the limits.

Naturally, the extent of the child's involvement in the limit-determining process must depend upon his age and maturity level. The older and more mature the child, the more direct involvement he should have. It is also crucial that both parents are in agreement since this is the only way to insure consistency and to provide both parents and children with the advantages of consistent behavior.

Earlier in this chapter the pitfalls of elastic limits were hinted at. What was said is true, but it is not equally true that the two extremes are the only alternatives. I believe in flexible limits, but please don't think this is a contradiction. I differentiate between elastic limits and flexible limits easily. Elastic limits are those which tend to stretch under pressure from an outside force. Generally they are inconsistently enforced according to mood.

Flexible limits, on the other hand, are open to change through negotiation between the parties involved. Situations and circumstances in life change, and when they do limits may need to be altered. This is reasonable, but it should be accomplished by the parent and the child through discussion and negotiation of some kind. For example, the younger and less mature the child, the tighter and more restrictive the limits probably will be. As the youngster grows and matures, the limits need to be expanded so as to encourage and enable the child to experience progress in his life. This point can be explained by a simple example:

An infant is usually confined to a crib, a carrier, or someone's arms before he can sit up. Before long the environment is expanded and the child is placed in a playpen—more room but still very tight limits. The child continues to grow and to become mobile and within a short time is placed on the floor—but with all doors shut. More growth and maturity bring as a consequence more free space in which the tot can move. Now the youngster has the run of the house, except the stairway and bathroom. Time passes, and even those limits are removed. Eventually, the child is taken outside where he is free to play, but within a fenced yard and likely under the constant observation of a responsible person. With the receipt of a wagon, scooter, or tricycle comes more freedom, but the corner or a neighbor's house represents the limits of travel. Later it is the two-wheeler to school and back, but it must be walked across the busy streets. And so it goes, until the child becomes sufficiently responsible to leave home for good and to be on his own.

The prototype of this kind of parenting can be recognized in the instructions given Adam and Eve by their Heavenly Parent while they were in the Garden of Eden. They were told of the situation they were in. The limits were made clear with specific consequences spelled out should the limits be violated: "Of every tree of the garden thou mayest freely eat, But of the tree of the knowledge of good and evil, thou shalt not eat of it," and then the consequences: "for in the day thou eatest thereof, thou shalt surely die." The Father also declared his position but left his children with their agency, "remember that I forbid it." But, "nevertheless, thou mayest choose for thyself." (Moses 3:16, 17.) The rest of the story is history. The limits were overstepped, and the specified consequences occurred. Parents, too, must learn to allow the consequences to occur.

The idea is to permit a child to have freedom with limits. This is a reality of life. You and I as adults must live within limits. Flexible and expandable limits allow the child to experience a sense of competency and growth. Without this opportunity, the child will not be able to mature as he should.

But a word of caution: Freedom within limits as described in this chapter is not the same as limitless freedom. It is not a permissive approach, but rather a responsible one. You see, the child soon learns one of the most valuable lessons in life: that there is more freedom for one who can handle it and less freedom for the individual who demonstrates the inability to make appropriate choices and decisions.

Consequences for the violation of limits are logical and simply result in the reduction of the limits. Such consequences are most effective when discussed in advance with the child. The child has the responsibility to behave in a manner consistent with the freedom he has been allowed. To fail to do so results in the loss of freedom. More detail about this can be found in the chapter "The More Control We Have From Within, the Less We Need From Without." Parents and their children should never forget that limits make freedom possible.

SUGGESTIONS:

1. Work together with your spouse on defining and setting limits. Consistency is extremely important for the welfare of the child.

2. Involve the child as much as you can in setting limits and deciding the resulting consequences for any violations. I realize this is not possible for everything but can assure you that the more it is done, the better things will go.

3. Frequently evaluate the limits and be open for change should that become necessary. The child should have the right (and the courage) to initiate negotiation for change as well as the parents.

4. Realize that your task is to train the child to get along without you at some point. The key is expanding responsibility.

5. Don't be afraid to restrict the limits if the child proves unable to handle that particular amount of freedom. You will be doing your child a favor.

13

The More Control We Have From Within, the Less We Need From Without

---

It honestly is no exaggeration to say that hundreds of parents have told me how helpful the adage "The more control we have from within, the less we need from without" has been for them. I know exactly why. It has been for me too. We have discussed and applied the concept of self-control so often in my own family that if anyone were to ask any of our children what the key word in our household is, each would answer without hesitation: "Control."

This word is as powerful as it is simple, and it proves itself time and again in a wide variety of situations.

In my profession I listen carefully to many people. I haven't met one yet who wants to be controlled. It is the same for any age, young or old. (Okay, there are a few exceptions, such as those who have been institutionalized to the point of not wanting to face the world on their own. But these are very few.)

Certainly a primary goal of parents is to help their child develop self-control. They know that critically important matters in life turn on an individual's being in or out of control. They want each child to assume responsibility for behavior and want that youngster to be motivated from within rather than being controlled or strongly influenced by others and by outside forces.

The concept we are considering suggests a process whereby any person can increase or decrease the amount of outside control needed by increasing or decreasing the amount of control he has within himself.

Here is a common example: Suppose I have demonstrated my internal control sufficiently to drive a car because I've passed the written and driving tests. When the state issues a license, the assumption is that I will maintain the control already exhibited. Now, suppose that someday I allow myself to become upset over something and lose enough self-control that I drive faster and faster. Before long I am pulled over by a policeman because I am driving out of control. Assume I merely get a warning ticket, and I smile. But as soon as he is out of sight, I begin driving recklessly (that is, out of control) again. If I keep this up, I will eventually lose my right to drive and will also forfeit a good deal of control over my own life in the process. If I am so out of control that I become a menace, society might even lock me up. The jails are full of people who do not have enough internal control to be loose.

All of us want to control our own lives. Children are no exception. The story about a mother and her four-year-old in a church service is right in point. The tot couldn't see over the head of the lady in front of him, so he stood up. Each time he did this his mother would sit him down gently but firmly. Her efforts were futile because the lad was soon up again, standing on the bench. When the mother finally lost her control, sat him down with a push, and warned him of the dire consequences should he choose to stand up again, he was frightened. Although physically controlled from without, he looked at his mother with a quivering lower lip and declared, "I'm sitting on the outside, but I'm standing on the inside." I repeat: No one really wants to be controlled.

The dislike of external control can be a powerful reinforcement for self-control, and parents should use this desire for freedom to good advantage. Suppose your teenager wants to go to a movie on a school night. You agree on condition that the youth control events so as to be home before 10:00 P.M. The young person understands the agreement. But since "time flies when you're having fun," he forgets the time (that is, loses control of it) and stays out until midnight.

Neither a sermon nor a physical lesson will give lasting results. What he does need is to suffer the logical consequences for having lost control on this occasion. Next time he asks to go out on a school night both parents must reply, "Not this time." He needs to know that the decision isn't made because they are angry with him or because they don't want him to have any fun, but because he previously demonstrated the lack of internal control necessary to be in charge of such a situation. He can only blame himself.

The parent isn't the bad guy or the heavy. The youth must learn that responsibility for one's behavior means self-control and that when it has been demonstrated in lesser matters (not necessarily for a fixed time period), he will be deserving of another try and the external controls will be loosened. The same process works equally well with younger children. The important thing is that they must understand the principle, the responsibility for self-control, and the resulting good or bad consequences.

Remember, this motto can be stated in two forms by interchanging the words *more* and *less*. My preference is to highlight the positive aspect rather than the negative one.

"Do you remember the key word?"

"*Control*."

"You've got it!"

SUGGESTIONS:

1. Make sure you and your children understand how this principle of self-control works. (*You* must apply it in your actions and reactions too.)

2. Write the word *control* on some pieces of paper and put the pieces around the house in conspicuous places.

3. Whenever external control must be used, be certain to

explain to the child that he is being controlled because he failed to have enough internal control at a particular time.

4. Compliment the child when internal control is demonstrated. Remember, rewarded behavior continues. Children need to become aware of this feeling, to be able to recognize it, and wish to repeat it.

14

Always Allow Alternatives

Before reading any further just now, please stop and try to remember the last time you were told what to do and what your reaction was when you realized you had neither voice nor choice in the matter.

I'll wager that it was not a positive experience for you because I can't imagine anyone who feels good in a situation which is entirely out of his control. Consider how much more negative it must be for children who have many fewer positive experiences in their emotional banks upon which to draw when they need good feelings. It is the very unusual person who doesn't want to have some say in his life. Most of us want to be able to make decisions and to influence the choices which affect us.

Emotionally healthy individuals, whether children, adolescents, or adults, seem to have three basic emotional needs in common. The first is a need to belong, to feel loved and to be an integral part of a larger group. The second is a need to be competent, the feeling of being able to do *something* better than others can, or at least as well as others can. The third emotional need is to feel useful, to have a feeling of personal value. People who possess these three feelings are considered to have positive self-esteem, that is, they feel good about themselves. As parents, we naturally want our children to have positive feelings about themselves.

One of the best guaranteed ways to foster positive self-esteem in children is to encourage and allow them to become involved in the decision-making processes for matters touching upon their own lives. A child who is asked his opinion about something in the family feels more a part of that family than before. It is difficult for anyone to develop the sense of belonging if he is constantly told what to do and not allowed any choice. Being able to make choices and to have input into discussions is perhaps the best proof that a person has a secure place in the group.

Just as being allowed to contribute to the making of choices enhances a person's sense of belonging, so does it increase his feeling of competence. If someone does everything for me, even makes all the decisions for me, I just about have to conclude that I am not capable of doing these things for myself. There is no real feeling of accomplishment if I only do what I've been told to do—even if the result is an outstanding success. I need to make some choices. Agency, i.e., the right to choose between alternatives, is an eternal principle.

The consequences of a parent's not allowing a child to make decisions and choices are seen in the life of a twenty-one-year-old girl I met in an institute class. This girl was struggling to survive living at home while being herself. She told the class that her mother insisted on making *all* the rules she was to follow as long as she was living at home. Quite literally, the mother made all the basic rules for the young lady. Apparently, it had been the same throughout her life.

After the class had been dismissed, she stayed on to talk with me. I want to quote as accurately as I can what she said about not having been given the opportunity to choose anything for herself: "My mother is always right and I am always wrong when we don't agree. Every time this happens I feel a little part of myself leave me—do you know what I mean? It's like I'm not capable of deciding anything. But my mother says I need to stay at home for awhile longer until I have enough money to go out on my own or get married." Even the decision to leave or stay home was being made by this mother. The young lady was a very immature twenty-one-year-old.

Unfortunately, I don't always follow my own advice to allow alternatives. I have analyzed why I sometimes do not allow my own children to choose between meaningful alternatives even when I know how important the process is. I suspect that I fail for the very same reasons that many other people do. Three reasons occurred to me as to why I don't always practice what I preach.

In the first place, setting up alternatives for choice takes time, and I always seem to be in a hurry. There are other things to be done, and it is much quicker to say: "Okay, it's time to get to your homework."

A second reason why is that it is easier to do the thinking for my boys. If *I* do the choosing, only *I* have to think of how *I* feel and what *I* think is right. To allow alternatives would involve having to put myself into the child's place and trying to feel how he probably feels.

A third reason why is that sometimes I simply can't think of meaningful alternatives at that moment, and I am not prepared to take the time or expend the energy to think some up.

Having recounted this, I must admit that whenever I fail to follow my own advice in the matter of alternatives, the reason is that I am either too selfish or more interested in the task I want done than in the emotional well-being of my child. In spite of these confessed lapses, I remain convinced that if parents and teachers will take the time to create and then present alternatives to the child, both they and the youngster will be more satisfied with the final results than if they do not.

The following basic principles will encourage everyone to always allow alternatives:

1. *The right to choose what we will or will not do is an eternal principle.* Agency was a matter of prime importance in the premortal

existence. Adam and Eve were free to choose in the Garden of Eden. Thus, each of us has been given the right of choice in all we do, and this God-given right should be enhanced by us mortals.

2. *The less mature the child, the fewer and simpler the alternatives should be.* A young child may do well to choose between two alternatives, while an adolescent can be capable of choosing among many.

For example, to take a very young child into a Thirty-one Flavors dispensary for an ice cream cone and tell him to choose *one* from all those available can be a very frustrating experience for him. If he is like boys I know, he would like to have one of each kind. It is better to indicate two or three flavors to the youngster, and then let him choose from among them. The same principle should be applied when a youngster has a room to clean, some homework to do, an errand to run, and the need to play. The order in which these are accomplished may not be important, provided all are completed by dark. If the child is quite young, the parent might limit alternatives by saying: "You can either clean your room first or run the errand, whichever you would like."

A ten-year-old might enjoy the challenge of setting priorities among all four activities. Even bedtime can be made a matter of choice if an effort is made to arrange alternatives. Suppose a parent feels strongly that the child must be in bed by 8:30 P.M. Instead of announcing that fact, the mother could say, "You can either go to bed at eight o'clock or eight-thirty, depending on how tired you feel." It is astonishing how often children will choose the earlier time because they have had the choice. It is no surprise that they will often fight even the later hour if they feel they are being forced. (After one of my more enthusiastic lessons on this principle in a parent-education class, a father came to me and said, "I took your advice and my child now has a choice about bedtime. I told him he can either go to bed smiling and happy, or crying with a spanking." The principle was right but something seemed a bit wrong about the alternatives!)

3. *Only allow alternatives you as a parent can live with.* If you present an alternative you don't really wish the child to choose, you will end up saying to the child, "You can choose"; and then after the

"wrong" choice is made, you have to take your offer back. Neither children nor adults like to be treated in this manner.

Here is an example one mother expressed to the class. She had been impressed with our discussions about allowing choices for children and wanted to put the principle into effect in her family. The next Saturday she took her eight-year-old daughter shopping for shoes. As they entered the store the mother announced to her daughter, "We will purchase any pair of shoes you want, as long as they fit."

First of all, the little girl was overwhelmed by all the shoe styles and colors and consequently was very frustrated. She finally chose a pair of purple shoes which were dainty, fragile, and expensive. The mother admitted she had been caught in her own trap. She had to go back on her word. The little girl was crushed and wouldn't even look at any of the other shoes. The ensuing scene was a disaster even though the mother's motives had been well intended. Had the mother initially selected two or three acceptable alternatives and then allowed the daughter to select the pair she desired, everyone involved would have been better off and they would have lived happily forever after, at least for the rest of that day.

4. *Allow the child to help create appropriate alternatives.* It is a good idea to allow children to share this growing experience. Their wisdom will often astound the parents. When a child is faced with a dilemma of some kind and asks the parent what to do, a wise parent may choose to respond, "Well, let's see what choices you have." Together they can create a suitable list of alternatives. If the child can learn this process at an early age, it will prove to be a valuable skill throughout life.

5. *Remember, freedom of choice means responsibility for behavior.* This principle has two dimensions: If there is no choice, a child will not feel responsibility for either positive or negative outcomes. If the choice turns out right, the parent earns the credit; if it turns out wrong, the parent deserves the blame. The child is released of all responsibility.

The other dimension, that of choice, is that if the child makes the decision, he must also assume the responsibility for whatever consequences occur. If the choice is a good one, he will feel positive about himself; if it turns out to have been a bad one, he will learn from the consequences which follow. Thus, choice becomes a happy, no-lose situation. The child grows, and that is what life is for.

It is important to reiterate that almost all parents really want what is best for their children. But parents often make mistakes when they feel that they know what the "best" is because they are the parents. They probably do, but if they force their superior knowledge on a child, they likely will be short-changed in the long run by getting compliance but not obedience. Force can result either in rebellion or compliance but never in obedience. Obedience is the result of choice. This concept will be more fully developed in another chapter.

We can see the importance of choice as we look at the way the Church has a balance of authority and individual rights. A priesthood holder is a free agent, and his capacity to be spiritual must be respected. As a leader he invites, persuades, encourages, and recommends in a spirit of gentleness and meekness. In this kind of atmosphere members respond freely as guided by the Spirit. Only this kind of response has moral value, for it arises out of knowledge, faith, love, or religious intent. It is contrary to God's gift of free agency to use fear and force as a means of attaining "obedience."

It seems to me that in the previous paragraph we can properly substitute the words *family* for *church* and *children* for *members* and thereby bring this concept of agency and responsibility into our home situations because the principles involved are true.

In summary, a parent will have more personal freedom and happier, healthier children when time and care are taken to present alternatives.

SUGGESTIONS:
    1. Whenever you want a child to do something, give him a

choice. A "Would you do this for me?" allows choice; a "Do it!" does not.

2. Discuss with the child not only the choices available but also the possible consequences of each choice.

3. Care enough about your child to let him make a wrong choice and work through the consequences which arise. (I realize there may be some consequences too drastic to allow to occur, but these are few and would have been taken into consideration when the alternatives were presented.)

4. Keep track of appropriate choices by your children, and I think you will be amazed at their wisdom.

5. Always have faith in your children.

15

Measure Twice, Cut Once

The two stories that follow, although seemingly quite unrelated at first reading, represent the extremes of a decision-making process.

Once upon a time a woodcutter and his wife lived in the forest and had as their only other companion a faithful dog. The three of them were very close to one another. As time passed the wife gave birth to a baby boy, and then there were four. The winds of fate were not kind and after a couple of years, the wife took ill and died of a fever.

The woodcutter decided to remain in the wilderness and would take his young son and his faithful dog along with him when he was out cutting wood.

One day he learned of the presence of a wolf and decided, for the safety of the child, to leave him and the dog at home for a few hours at a time. He checked and double-checked all the doors before leaving just to be sure.

While he was gone, the wolf did come to the little home and, finding a back window open, slipped inside. The dog heard the noise and immediately took the sleeping youth by the shirt and pushed him behind the couch in the front part of the cabin. Then the dog went into the back room to do battle with the intruder. After a long and hard fight, the wolf fell dead at the feet of the panting, sweating dog. The dog quickly went back to his watching position and fell asleep.

The woodcutter returned home. As he opened the door his nose caught the scent of the perspiration. He saw the room in disarray, but his child was nowhere to be seen. It was then he noticed the dog, lying there still wet from perspiration and with blood stains around his jaws. Without looking further, the wood-cutter judged what had happened: The dog had gone mad and had killed the child. Without further thought, he raised his axe high above his head and buried it deep into the skull of his favorite dog and faithful companion.

The yelp of the dog awoke the sleeping child who then called out to his father. The child was not harmed; so where did the blood come from? Upon investigation the father found the dead wolf, and then he knew what his hasty judgment had cost him. But it was too late.

The second story is about a ten-year-old lad who thought he knew more about his pet dog than anyone else. Oh, how he loved his furry friend! He couldn't stand to see any harm come to him.

One night his father announced that the tail of the dog needed to be cut off for the sake of cleanliness. The son pleaded, but to no avail. The father really believed this was the best thing to do and finally convinced the boy. The child's only request was that he be allowed to do it.

Since the father was leaving town, he showed the boy how short the tail should be and instructed the boy how to accomplish this unpleasant task without risking the life of the animal. The boy said he understood and the father left town.

The boy, in an attempt to make his task less painful for the dog, decided not to cut the whole tail off at once. He chose, instead, to cut it off an inch every day.

Terrible stories, aren't they? I'm glad they're not true. But they do point out the significance of this particular proverb. You see, the woodcutter represents the parent who reacts with emotion rather than reason when certain situations occur. No one can think very clearly when he is emotional. The young boy in the second story, on the other hand, represents those parents, who in an effort to be more kind to a child, actually prolong the pain and make a bad situation worse than it has to be. Obviously both extremes result in greater problems. The key seems to be a balance between our feelings and our thoughts.

There is a big difference—a very big one—between a parent acting on a situation and a parent reacting to a situation. The former suggests internal control while the latter indicates the lack of such control. Emotions tend to confuse the issues at hand. Parents simply must always think before acting if they are to protect the emotional welfare of the child, and themselves for that matter.

Thomas Jefferson rightly stated, "Delay is preferable to error." Granted, there are times when a parent must respond immediately to the situation at hand. Those times, however, are relatively few and far between. Generally there is not that urgency, and the wise parent will learn as much as possible about the situation before passing judgment and handing down the sentence.

Suppose your child embarrasses you in front of your friends and needs some disciplinary action. Both parent and child will be better off if time is allowed to pass and cooler heads prevail. Think it through and then act precisely. As the motto reads, "Measure twice and cut once." One advantage of two parents is that they can consult with one another and help clear up any misunderstandings. One parent can and should calm the other if need be.

A final point should be emphasized: Once your mind is made up as to the appropriate action, it should be done. Postponing it or trying to make it softer will usually backfire.

One thing is certain: Whatever is done must be done in love. This is the real key.

SUGGESTIONS:

1. Repeat the word *control* in your mind when you feel yourself heating up.

2. Find someone to talk to if you feel your emotions are in charge.

3. Except in an emergency, make it a policy to never decide at once. Even a five-minute wait may be worth a lot to you and to the child.

4. Decide in advance, whenever possible, the consequences which logically follow any particular misbehavior. This may appear to be a little idealistic, but it is often quite possible.

5. Before reacting, ask yourself this question: "Will this behavior get me where I want to go with my child?" If not, find another way to handle it.

16

What Isn't Talked Out Will Likely Be Acted Out

A short time ago when driving through the beautiful White Mountains of northern Arizona, I became completely captivated by the beauty of the changing leaves. I have never seen brighter yellows and oranges nor seen autumn so picturesque. Quite suddenly, I noticed my eyes were wet and even felt a teardrop roll down my cheek. I know my feelings are often very close to the surface, but this seemed a bit too emotional even for me. After the initial surprise at my emotion, I realized the reason for the tears: I was alone in the car. There was no one with whom I could share this joyous feeling. I wished from my deepest heart that my wife could have been there. It seemed like a terrible waste not to have been able to share this feeling with her. I do not envy the person who is alone too much of the time.

Everyone has strong feelings, and very often they wish to share them. These feelings might be either positive or negative. Happiness is increased when shared, and sadness seems less burdensome if there is someone to help carry it. An old German proverb is exactly to the point: Shared joy is double joy and shared sorrow is half sorrow.

Sometimes our desire to share feelings with others comes from a strong urge to be helpful. We think that we can say something to a particular individual which will be profitable. However, whether or not we take the next step and actually express those personal feelings and thoughts depends to a large degree on the relationship which exists between us and the person involved. If we believe our words will be accepted as intended, we will be more likely to say them. If, however, we are fearful of how the other will react, or if we cannot predict what will happen if we say what we are thinking, we find it difficult to expose those personal feelings which are deep inside us.

There are, of course, those times when our feelings are so intense that we don't care what the outcome of our conversation is, and we just "let 'er fly." One gem of New Testament wisdom brings into focus how we should convey our thoughts to another person. Paul admonishes us to "speak the truth in love." Whatever we have to say ought to be designed to strengthen and heal, not hurt or destroy.

In order to truly share deep feelings, one must develop a trusting relationship with others. To accomplish this involves being both willing and able to share feelings, as well as working to create an atmosphere of understanding and acceptance. Then the two people involved can open their hearts to one another. This need is especially real among family members. Friends come and go, but families are part of an eternal association.

Adults (parents) have some definite advantages over children in the matter of sharing feelings. Because they have had more experiences in life, adults are aware of several different ways of saying whatever is on their mind as well as being more expert in predicting what the likely outcome of their statements will be. Children usually lack a stock of experiences and the sensitivity to watch for reactions. In addition, adults are naturally more in control of situations and so have greater power within the relationship.

Another advantage available to parents is a wider variety of ways to work off frustration and anger when they arise. Adults may leave the scene, take a brisk walk, or slam a tennis ball. Because they have more advantages, parents also have more responsibility in achieving that wonderful relationship of sharing feelings with their child. Both negative as well as positive emotions should be shared. When feelings are shared in love, positive feedback will reinforce what has gone on, and constructive negative feedback will motivate change.

Problems can develop if a parent sends an emotional message to a child to which the child feels unable (for whatever reason) to respond verbally. The concept of this chapter is that the child *will* respond—if not verbally then behaviorally to such messages.

For example, suppose you decide that your eleven-year-old daughter is taking too long in the shower. Although you are irritated about the situation, the girl apparently doesn't respond to your indirect comments. You gently but firmly tell her to hurry up and not to use so much hot water. At that particular time she has many other things on her mind (the new boy who just moved in down the street). Besides, she thinks she is old enough for a grown-up-shower-time allotment and resents being treated like a child.

If she is unable to tell you how she feels and/or is fearful of the consequences she thinks will occur if she does, she says nothing. She will, however, manage to get water all over the floor and to break a bottle of shampoo. The interesting thing about this type of reaction is that usually the child is not consciously aware of why she does things like these. But you will get her message.

Or, another example: Perhaps you inform your seventeen-year-old that he will not be able to take the family car to the movie on Saturday as planned. He has learned not to enter into an argument with you about it, but you notice he is wearing his grubbies to school the next day. He happens to know how embarrassed you get when he dresses like this.

If a child would merely find a way to lash out at a parent, not too much damage is done. The danger is that he might also take out his anger on himself. Quitting a much-needed job, telling a good friend to get lost, or even suicide attempts may stem from unspoken anger. Physical symptoms such as ulcers, migraine head-aches, and breathing difficulties can often be attributed to repressed emotions.

The extreme of this condition can be illustrated by a simple analogy. Think about a teakettle on a stove, filled with water and the plate turned to high heat. Teakettles are made with a safety valve which opens to let the steam escape rather than build up and create tremendous pressure. Ponder for a moment what would happen if the safety valve were to remain shut. An ensuing explosion is inevitable unless the heat is turned off, the water allowed to cool, or the valve opened.

So it is with children. It is extremely important that they keep a safety valve open and functioning. They need to feel safe in their environment to the point that they can express their thoughts appropriately and should be taught by example as well as with words how this can be done so as to create as little defensiveness as possible in the other person. If little feelings are not dealt with, they tend to grow and to expand into big feelings.

The situation comes to mind of a man who, while walking in the desert, was bitten by a poisonous snake. After he realized he actually had been bitten, there were three basic choices open to him: First, he could, if he so chose, allow himself to become very angry and emotionally upset at the snake. Filled with hate and seeking revenge, he might then grab the nearest stick and go after the snake. The end result would be a quicker death for him as well. Second, he literally could tell himself he had not been bitten and so do nothing about the poison in his system. Again, the end result likely would be death, but this time it would take a bit longer. A third alternative would be to find some way of getting the poison out of his system and/or ingesting something to counteract the effect of the venom. Should he make such a choice, he probably would live to hike another day.

Talking out one's problems or frustrations is to take the third alternative of getting the poison out of the system. In addition, ingesting the acceptance and understanding of a good listener is a powerful antidote for many emotional poisons.

Please understand that I am not suggesting that a child be allowed, without consequence, to tell others whatever he chooses in any situation or at any given time. We are concerned with sharing, sensitivity, and love. Some people justify their rudeness and selfishness in the name of emotional honesty, but they should reflect on these very insightful words written by Dr. James Dobson: "Honesty which does not have the best interest of the hearer at heart is a cruel form of selfishness." (*What Wives Wish Their Husbands Knew About Women* [Wheaton, Ill: Tyndale House, 1975], p. 41.)

What I am suggesting is that children be encouraged to interact with their parents, to negotiate with them, to share feelings together often (and always when necessary). If a child is allowed and taught how to express his displeasure, the matter often ceases to be displeasurable to him. The child needs to know that such feelings are fine, but that all of us must learn the appropriate ways to deal with them. If he feels he and his parents can't talk these feelings out, he will likely resort to acting out his emotions.

SUGGESTIONS:

1. Help the child recognize and accept angry feelings as natural by talking about the process and being willing to share feelings of your own as examples. When a child experiences your willingness to deal openly with feelings, he will be more likely to do so.

2. Legitimize the child's feelings. Don't try to tell him that he doesn't feel a certain way. He does feel it, right or wrong. Remember, it isn't the *feeling* that is bad; it is the way the feeling is *managed* that can be bad. Respect the feeling of the child. Help him to feel accepted, whatever his feelings are.

3. Teach children ways to express feelings without offending others. Teach them to describe behavior rather than people, to be tentative rather than rigid in what they say.

17

He Who Angers Me
Controls Me

As a young child I was fascinated by and even dreamed of becoming a ventriloquist. Once I even got as far as the public library to search for a book or two to help me realize this goal. I never did locate such a book, and because I never pursued this particular idea far enough, the conclusion must be that my interest was more of a fantasy than a desire.

I am, however, still fascinated by the skill and art of a good ventriloquist and conclude there must be a lot more people like me because of the enormous popularity of the Muppet productions. Each of these personalities seem to be as much alive as did the dummies of the ventriloquists when I was a child. One of the greatest of these, Edgar Bergen, stated on one occasion that the reason for his phenomenal success was the genuineness of his characters, Charlie McCarthy and Mortimer Snerd. People identified with them just as they now do with Kermit and Miss Piggy and all the rest. And who could ever forget little Pinocchio? Could I ever identify with him! In my younger days I still remember reaching up to feel if *my* nose were growing longer a few times.

Now, in all this imagery, let me point out that I wanted to be the ventriloquist and not the dummy. Most of us would prefer to be the puppeteer rather than the puppet. It would be a terrible thing to be completely and totally controlled from the outside. The prospect of someone else pulling the strings; of not being able to set your own goals; of not determining your own pace in working toward those goals; or, in short, of not being able to decide for yourself in the varied aspects of living is a kind of slavery few of us could endure. It is difficult to think of an existence less satisfying and more frustrating than not being in control of what could be said or done.

This, however, is exactly what happens to those who allow themselves to become angry. This is because anger is an emotional reaction to a given condition. It is a secondary rather than a primary emotion because anger grows out of some other feeling. Anger results from such primary emotions as feeling hurt, frustrated, belittled, and so on, if these primary emotions are not dealt with quickly and decisively. Since anger is a reaction which displaces reason, the angry person can only *react* to whatever and/or whomever is causing the anger. Reacting, of course, is like being a puppet on a string. Cues are taken from the controller, and the controlled gives up power to choose a particular behavior.

Most of us are familiar with the truth of this observation since at one time or another in our lives we have let anger force out reason. For example, it is easy to put yourself in this position if you haven't already experienced it: While driving down a street minding your own business and feeling at peace with the world, a thoughtless driver cuts in front of you, requiring you to react by slamming on your brakes. As your tires squeal and your car lurches, it is easy to spout words you never thought were in your own vocabulary. You really don't want to talk like that or even think the thoughts that occur to you, but *fear* has suddenly grown into anger and you reacted to it.

If you yell loudly enough, and/or lay on your horn heavily enough, the perpetrator of the evil deed—the inconsiderate driver in the car which led to your reaction—will probably respond in a similar manner, with the additional noise and some nonverbal behavior which demonstrates his anger because of your anger. All of us have read of people actually being killed or badly battered over such a trivial, yet familiar situation. This occurs because anger robs us of control, and a person out of control can be dangerous.

When I think of how I have behaved when angry, and recall the regrettable things I have said or done after having lost reasoning power to anger, I can better understand why the Savior made such a point about it in his Sermon on the Mount. The fifth chapter of Matthew talks very directly about the need for us to control our emotions. The Savior even suggests that we leave our gifts at the altar and seek reconciliation before proceeding with the ordinance. In verse twenty-five of that same chapter we read how problems spiral when anger is not controlled.

We all learned in early childhood how much more quickly healing came when the injury was treated promptly. Some of us even may have learned to our regret how problems grew in severity—including infection and pain—when injuries were not taken care of quickly.

Cool heads are particularly important in parenting. Reacting with anger seldom, if ever, solves problems. The counsel of Ecclesiastes 7:9 ought to be one of the first entries in any how-to-be-a-parent book. It says very clearly what happens to one who loses emotional control by becoming angry: "Be not hasty in thy spirit to be angry: for anger resteth in the bosom of fools."

How can an angry (righteously, of course) parent be a fool? For certain one of the things children learn very early in life is which button to push in order to upset others, especially parents. Ordinarily, if a goal of a child is to upset the parent, he knows exactly how to do it by violating a value or principle known to be dear to the adults concerned. If attendance and performance at school are important to the parents, any child can manage to fail or do very poorly. If wearing hair short is a value to the parents a child may insist upon letting his grow. A girl may deliberately choose to dress immodestly, adopt profane expressions, or think up any number of behaviors designed to lead her parents to lose control of their emotions.

The reason why is as well understood as it is true: If children get the parents upset and angry, then the children will be in control. Children are not always deliberate about this, and often are not at all aware of their real motives. In fact, the motive is more often on the subconscious level. Thus, what they do may not be deliberate but it is always purposeful.

The purpose would be specific to the situation but would very probably fall into one of three general categories: (1) to get attention, (2) to demonstrate power, or (3) to hurt someone in order to get revenge. The child achieves the purpose of his actions if the parent falls into the trap and, by becoming emotional and losing reasoning power, responds like a puppet. Once control is lost and things are said or done in anger, it is the child, not the parent, who is in charge. Hence the motto, "He who angers me, controls me." It is not surprising that parents who react to provocation with anger will certainly reinforce the misbehavior of that child. As you know, rewarded behavior continues.

Therefore, in order to be in control, one must retain rationality and keep the thought processes in good working order. This means dealing with primary feelings before they culminate in anger. To do otherwise is to turn control over to the adversary. It is good counsel, indeed, never to argue with a fool—if only because people may have trouble telling which one is the fool.

SUGGESTIONS:

1. Recognize anger as a secondary emotion and learn to deal with whatever feeling precedes it.

2. Develop and use some strategy, such as deep breathing, counting to ten, or reciting a particular verse to keep your emotional level down.

3. Learn to express your feelings in a calm, unthreatening manner. I recommend the verse in Ephesians 4:15 wherein Paul admonishes us to speak the truth in love. Certainly our feelings should be expressed, but the motive and manner for expressing our feelings are of utmost importance.

4. Resolve to remain in control of your life and choose not to react angrily.

5. Plan in advance how you desire to handle situations you have found upsetting in the past. You can probably learn how to avoid some of these.

6. Withdraw from an interaction until the emotions are under control. Calling time out, as if in some athletic contest, may save the situation. If you utilize this method, however, be sure you don't forget to come back to the game. A time out doesn't mean the game is over.

18

A Stitch in Time Saves Nine

There is a celebrated lawsuit pending against two members of the medical profession. The plaintiffs are maintaining that their beloved husband and father is dead because both doctors failed to make an accurate diagnosis. It is purported that the physicians diagnosed the man's symptoms as valley fever (an illness somewhat indigenous to the Phoenix Valley, I understand) and prescribed treatment accordingly. In this case, the medication apparently was useless and the symptoms grew more pronounced. After several months and an examination by another physician, a malignancy was discovered. By this time the cancer cells were so widespread that the case was declared terminal, and a few months later the man died.

The suit contends that had the two doctors made the correct diagnosis at the outset, the cancer likely could have been arrested during that early stage. No one will ever know, but the point of the story is clear. Problems generally are more easily solved when confronted at an early stage. In the case of this tragedy, awareness of the real problem, cancer, came too late.

Most of us can relate instances wherein "a stitch in time" would have "saved nine." For example, I recall the time we purchased a new car and determined to take extra good care of it. One day I noticed a small hole in the back of the front seat. I told myself, "I had better get some liquid vinyl and repair that tear while it is small." Unfortunately, procrastination is one of my most frequently used self-defeating behaviors. I simply did not get around to fixing the hole. Before long, the hole became a small tear and then a long three- to four-inch rip. By then it was so large that any attempt to repair it on my own would have resulted in a messy job. Had I gotten to that hole when it first became apparent, it would have cost less to fix than two dollars. The cheapest bid I have to date is thirty dollars. In this particular instance, a patch in time may well have saved twenty-eight dollars.

The same principle applies in confronting the problems we find with our youngsters. Quite often the problem either seems too trivial to worry about, or else we jump to some erroneous conclusions as to the cause and then fail to treat it properly. There are times we yield to the temptation of closing our eyes and pretending we don't see the problem—all the while hoping it will take care of itself. I am frequently reminded of this when I hear the words to a popular song, "There are none so blind, as those who will not see." The truth is that we often refuse to see because we don't know what we'll do with what we find.

I'm suggesting that parents need to be alert to the problems their children may be experiencing, and they should deal with these situations as early as possible. I don't mean to be totally pessimistic, but sometimes by the time an older teenager is brought in to see a professional counselor, the illness has almost reached the inoperable or terminal state. Had efforts been made earlier to work on a particular problem it could have been resolved more successfully.

There are three basic steps I recommend for your consideration:

1. Parents should be alert and aware of developing problems.

While parents should not expect a child to misbehave, it is realistic to anticipate misbehavior. There is an important difference between the words *expect* and *anticipate.* When we *expect* something to occur, we generally commit ourselves to a reaction. We begin to act as if the thing were already happening. Oftentimes premature reactions actually encourage the unwanted behavior.

One particular instance comes to mind: A sixteen-year-old girl, who had become intimately involved with her boyfriend, had just learned of her pregnancy when she came to see me. She was terrified, angry, hurt, and confused over the situation. She had been to her bishop and had begun the process of repentance, but she was still very depressed. As we talked, she indicated that she and her boyfriend had been immoral only a few times. She said she had never intended to get involved in that way, but she had become so hurt and angry at her father, with all his insinuations that she just decided, as the old English saying goes, "To have the game as well as the blame." Her words to me went something like this: "I was accused of doing wrong things so many times, I actually began to feel guilty. Then one night, after having been called several really bad names by my dad, I just decided if I were going to be found guilty all the time, I might as well enjoy it."

Consequently, that very night she called her boyfriend, they met and she lost her virtue. I am not attempting to excuse her behavior. She did what she chose to do and must suffer the consequences. But we, as parents, need to be careful of the labels with which we tag our children. Our children very often will live up to or down to our expectations.

I remember a young teenage boy who was picked up for shoplifting. His nickname was Sneaky. Certainly you get the same message he was getting each and every day from his family. Time and experience have shown that many of us tend to behave in a manner consistent with what we think others expect of us. This phenomenon can work both positively and negatively, depending, of course, on the expectation. If, however, we anticipate a particular behavior, we are alert to the situation, flexible because we are uncommitted, and able to prepare for what we think might result.

Parents should be alert to such clues as sudden or prolonged mood changes, dramatic differences in eating and sleeping, and new and different friends. Parents should not overreact to isolated behaviors—anyone can have a bad day or be in a bad place at any given time. But if a change persists, it should be looked into.

Because stealing is a behavioral problem in some families, parents would do well to notice the existence of unexplained articles around the house. One mother, who came with her son after he had been caught and taken to court for stealing several bicycles, claimed she had never noticed the several (seven to be exact) bicycles in their back yard. The boy would steal the bikes, dismantle them, and sell the parts right out of his own yard. Remember to be constantly alert to patterns, but don't overreact to a single clue.

2. Once a problem has been noticed and tracked down, a parent needs to be honest by acknowledging and accepting the reality of the situation. Denial of a particular problem will never help resolve it. I remember the situation in which a seventeen-year-old girl came home one day and tearfully announced to her parents she was pregnant. The mother's response was classic. She simply, but emphatically, said, "You can't be! I won't have it in this family!" And that was the end of that conversation. The mother's denial did not change the condition of the girl. It is only after we acknowledge and accept a situation as being real, that we find the motivation to work on it.

3. The final step is to act appropriately. This can seldom be accomplished on an impulse. Most problems we face took time to develop and another few minutes' delay usually won't cause much additional damage. If we catch the problem early enough, the situation should be less emotional (for example, dealing with sexual misconduct is easier and less emotional than dealing with an unwanted pregnancy). Hence, there will be a greater possibility for both parents and child to work it out. Usually the longer we delay action, the more difficult it is to implement. We must find the happy medium, and this will usually be dictated by the personality of the child and the severity of the situation. In an earlier chapter

we discussed the Savior's admonition to "agree with thine adversary quickly" (Matthew 5:25). Situations are simply more effectively dealt with if noticed and handled before they develop into huge problems.

This motto could also have been written: "An ounce of prevention is worth a pound of cure." Rehabilitation will never match prevention. Surgery at its best is not going to repair a body part to the point of being better than the original, healthy tissue. While working as a teacher and counselor at a juvenile institution, I became very much concerned about setting up an effective prevention program. In one of my initial speeches to convince the powers that were, I recited a poem. Since then it has become a favorite of mine.

A Fence or an Ambulance

'Twas a dangerous cliff, as they freely confessed,
Though to walk near its crest was so pleasant.
But over its terrible edge there had slipped
A Duke and full many a peasant.
So the people said something would have to be done,
But their projects did not at all tally;
Some said, "Put a fence around the edge of the cliff,"
Some, "An ambulance down in the valley."

But the cry for the ambulance carried the day,
For it spread through the neighboring city;
A fence may be useful or not, it is true,
But each heart became brimful of pity
For those who slipped over that dangerous cliff.
And the dwellers in highway and alley
Gave pounds or gave pence, not to put up a fence,
But an ambulance down in the valley.

"For the cliff is all right, if you're careful," they said.
"And, if folks even slip and are dropping,
It isn't the slipping that hurts them so much,

As the shock down below when they're stopping."
So day after day, as these mishaps occurred,
Quick forth would those rescuers sally
To pick up the victims who fell off the cliff,
With their ambulance down in the valley.

Then an old sage remarked: "It's a marvel to me,
That people give far more attention
To repairing results than to stopping the cause,
When they'd much better aim at prevention.
Let us stop at its source all this mischief," cried he,
"Come, neighbors and friends, let us rally;
If the cliff we will fence we might almost dispense
With the ambulance down in the valley."

"Oh, he's a fanatic," the others rejoined,
"Dispense with the ambulance? Never!
He'd dispense with all charities, too, if he could;
No! No! We'll support them forever.
Aren't we picking up folks just as fast as they fall?
And shall this man dictate to us? Shall he?
Why should people of sense stop to put up a fence,
While the ambulance works in the valley?"

But a sensible few, who are practical too,
Will not bear with such nonsense much longer;
They believe that prevention is better than cure,
And their party will soon be the stronger.
Encourage them then, with your purse, voice, and pen,
And while other philanthropists dally,
They will scorn all pretense and put up a stout fence
On the cliff that hangs over the valley.

Better guide well the young than reclaim them when old,
For the voice of true wisdom is calling.
"To rescue the fallen is good, but 'tis best
To prevent other people from falling."
Better close up the source of temptation and crime

Than deliver from dungeon or galley;
Better put a strong fence round the top of the cliff—
Than an ambulance down in the valley.

— Joseph Malins

SUGGESTIONS:

1. Be alert and aware of problems. *Anticipate,* but don't *expect* them.

2. Acknowledge and accept the existing problem.

3. Act accordingly to resolve it. Working with the child has proven time and time again to be a very valuable step in diverting unacceptable behavior.

19

Walk to the End of the Light

The story is told of a nine-year-old boy who lived on a farm some distance from town and any neighbors. One night just before bedtime he remembered he had forgotten to close the gate out by the road. He knew this was his responsibility, but it was dark outside and he was very much afraid. The more his father insisted he go out and take care of his duty, the more frightened he became. On this particular night his father was ill and couldn't leave his bed. The boy knew he was the only one who could take care of the gate but the fear of darkness and of the unknown was almost paralyzing.

Finally the father decided on a plan. He had his son open the father's bedroom window which faced the gate. He gave the boy a flashlight and told him to use it to light his way to the gate. The boy stood on the doorstep for some time before moving at all. Then he heard his father's voice through the open window. "Ronnie, can you shine your light on the swing in the old oak tree?" the father asked.

"Yes," Ronnie answered.

"Then," said the father, "walk to the swing."

This the lad did. He heard his father's voice again. "Ronnie, can you see the corner of the barn?"

Ronnie held the light in the direction of the barn and then responded, "Yes, I can see it."

"Go to the end of the light," the father encouraged.

Once there, the boy heard his father's third question, "Now, can you see the tool shed?"

Ronnie focused the light on the tool shed. When he could see it, he answered, "Yes," and the father told him to walk to it. Once there, Ronnie knew what to do, and he shined the light in the direction of the open gate. Now he could see it within his light and he proceeded to walk to it and close it. He accomplished his return trip to the house in the same manner but in reverse. The key was going to the end of the light. This way he was never really in darkness.

Another example of this proverb comes to mind as I reflect back on my own early childhood. We, too, lived in a small town, and I was both frightened and amazed at how my father could drive a car at night on those unlighted, winding roads outside of town. He seemed to have radar of some kind because he stayed right on the road, a road that I couldn't even see. I didn't ever ask him how he did it, I only knew he could. It wasn't until I was becoming old enough to drive that I figured out the key. As a child I had tried to see beyond the headlights of the car. As a result, all I saw was the blackness of the night. The secret was to drive to the end of the light.

In a book of puzzles I had purchased to challenge the thinking processes of one of our sons, I found this thought-provoking question: "Is it easier to ride a bicycle up a long, steep hill at night or in the daytime?" "And why is this so?" It seemed to me that the answer was too obvious. We were living in Mesa, Arizona. It was summer, and the daytime temperatures were around 110 degrees. Certainly it would be easier to ride up a hill at night. Well, as it turned out, my answer was correct, but the reason was not. The author explained. "It is easier to ride a bicycle up a long, steep hill at night because you can only see to the end of your light. You are therefore less discouraged because you can't see the whole hill."

Perhaps you have already made the application of these analogies to parenting. If by chance you haven't, consider the following ideas: Many times our frustrations and fears of child rearing come because we tend to look beyond the light. We worry about our four-year-old attending school two years from now. We just know our little freckled-faced ten-year-old girl will never get any dates. It's even more obvious to us that the twelve-year-old will never graduate from high school. You see, we are worrying about the gate because it is out of our sight; we are trying to drive ahead of the headlights of the car. We must learn to "go to the end of the light" and then we will find that the light will illuminate our path another manageable stretch down the road.

We simply must adapt ourselves to raising our children one day at a time. This is not to say that we should have no concern about the future, but rather that there is a big difference between worrying about and planning for what lies ahead. Perhaps you remember how, as a sixth grader, you thought it would be impossible to ever learn algebra the way your ninth-grade brother was doing. Then, as a ninth grader, you ended up doing better in the subject than he did. It was Earl Nightingale who defined success as "the *progressive* realization of a worthy goal" (emphasis added). Patience and perseverance are the keys.

Perhaps this is the concept the Lord had in mind when he gave the Prophet Joseph the following counsel regarding the translation process: "Do not run faster or labor more than you have strength and means provided to enable you to translate; but be diligent unto the end." (D & C 10:4.)

Fear of the unknown and of the bugaboos invented by the imagination can be very debilitating. We literally can freeze in our tracks. I am acquainted with a newly married couple who have decided not to have children because they are sure the world will either be in terrible shape or nonexistent by the time any of their children would grow up. We even read news articles of parents who murder their children to protect them from the future. These types of actions only guarantee failure. Any twenty-mile hike is taken one step at a time. When we reach the end of the light, we find it will direct us ahead that much further.

It isn't accidental that the Holy Bible admonishes us to "Walk in the light." (1 John 1:7.)

SUGGESTIONS:

1. Analyze your personal fears relative to children, and determine how many of the fears are actually "beyond the light."

2. Determine short-range goals—goals within your reach—and strive toward their realization, one at a time.

3. Keep strong batteries in your "flashlights" and continually recharge them by remembering successes you have already achieved rather than weakening them by dwelling on negative experiences.

4. As you walk with your children, recognize that the shorter the legs, the shorter the stride.

20

Enjoy the Trip

Life is a journey. Most of us hope it will be a long one and that we will be accompanied by kindred souls throughout all of it. Logically, we should regard the smaller subtrips within life's journey the same way.

Nevertheless, taking a long trip, anything more than a couple of hours, with six of us in a mid-sized car never used to be a positive experience. It seemed as if the more the congestion, the more the contention. We lived in northern Utah, and my folks were in southern California, a distance of perhaps seven hundred miles. This was far enough to discourage frequent visits but close enough for an annual vacation or two. We made the journey several times and certainly enjoyed ourselves once we were there and again once we were home. We did not, however, relish the long hours in the car.

One time, however, was different—the trip over the desert and through those frustrating small towns was an exciting one. What made the difference? We found the secret of enjoying the trip. In the past we had been only destination minded. To us the important thing had been to *arrive* rather than to *travel*. We owe a debt of gratitude to my parents for this great discovery.

Here's how it came about. My parents had been in Utah about a month before our scheduled vacation to their home on the coast. On their return trip, my mother and father noted over 120 various points of interest. Mother would write down such things as "find a rock waterfall on the right side of the road," or "find the school building with the construction date of 1907 on it." My parents sent these sheets back to us, and we followed them on our trip later. Our children were very excited to spot the items on the list. The trip time seemed as if cut in half; and for the first time we actually enjoyed the traveling. Both mother and father commented later how this exercise had made their own return trip much more interesting as well. By the way, on the way home we not only followed their instructions in reverse but added several of our own to share with a sister and her family who were planning to make the same trip later.

You certainly see the point of this chapter: If we concentrate only on our destination, we can feel good and successful only once. If, however, we find ways to enjoy the entire trip, we continuously find satisfaction and recognize the many interesting points along the way. Much too often we decide against taking a little side trip because all we can think of is getting to where we are going.

Having children and rearing them is certainly an exciting journey, filled with moment-by-moment experiences. Yet so many times we look only at the destinations. For example, suppose one of our young ones has a significant part in the next elementary-school drama production. If we think only of the performance, we likely will find all the preparations and practicing tedious and tiring. Our enjoyment is limited only to the evening of the presentation. Then, if we are worn out by the "trip," we may even sleep through the performance, thus enjoying none of the experience. Someone has said, "For those who learn to enjoy the moment, there is never total failure."

There is yet another aspect of this saying which is equally significant: Unlike a journey on foot or in a car which can be repeated at a later date, once a moment in the life of a parent or a child is gone, it will never return. We truly will never pass this way again. One evening our boys had some friends over to watch TV and play games. When my wife and I returned home, things were slowing down a bit and we thought it might give the evening a boost by getting some of the old tape recordings out of the closet. For about an hour, we all enjoyed listening to our children's voices and concerns from as long as fifteen years before. It was exciting to relive those early years and experiences. The sad thing is that we stopped enjoying those tapes for several years in between. Like too many people in this world, we just became too busy with life to really enjoy life. Now I regret not having continued making tapes during all the years the children were growing up.

We need to take the time and make the effort to enjoy each day of our lives. It goes by all too quickly. The Christmas holidays furnish a familiar example: If our total concern is for that one particular morning, we miss all the joys of getting ready for it. The day comes and goes in an instant, never to return.

Children are only young once. We need to find the joy and excitement in the maturation process of each child. There is an important by-product: Children will share more of their lives with us if they sense our sustained enjoyment and interest in their developing lives.

There is another application of the proverb. So many older teenagers and young adults become frustrated in their dating experiences because they spend the entire evening worrying about whether or not they will have a good time, or worrying about whether there will be a goodnight kiss. Or perhaps they are overly concerned about the possibility of a future date.

Many times our worrying about having a good time gets in the way of our having a good time. The real key to a successful date is to learn to enjoy each moment—to enjoy the anticipation of the date, to enjoy getting ready for the date, to enjoy the sights and sounds of the evening and so on. To be only destination minded in a dating situation is to miss most of the excitement.

One final point, my wife and I are looking forward to the day when our children are gone from the home and are out on their own. I don't think it is wrong to want to be alone again. But it would surely be detrimental to the eternal family if that were all we were concentrating on. We really do enjoy living with our children, and our time together is passing all too quickly. I hear, however, that grandchildren also provide fun and excitement for special trips.

SUGGESTIONS:

1. Keep a daily journal of those moments as each child grows up. (Film and recordings make great record keepers.)

2. Learn to recognize the special times along the road of life and point them out to the children.

3. Force yourself to take time for some side trips. You'll get where you are going soon enough.